Praise for the Author

Belinda Joyce's *Survive and Enjoy Your Baby* book was invaluable to both of us before our baby was born and also as a quick reference point during those first few daunting months.

I found that the book had the perfect amount of personal experience mixed in with professional knowledge. It seemed to take the 'scary' out of what I needed to absorb and humanised the learning in very simple terms.

Belinda's knowledge and experience is extensive in all areas of baby and new mother care. Her chapter on what is essential to purchase and what is not was really helpful when on a budget as there are so many items marketed towards new parents that are unnecessary. We continue to use the book as a reference point and believe it will help us raise a healthy and happy baby.

– Mandy and Scott Jackman

Belinda has written a wonderful book, providing Australian families with up to date and very knowledgeable information. There was certainly a gap in the Australian market. The foundations of Belinda's experience both as a mother and professionally, makes this a great tool to assist families on their parenthood journeys.

– Ali Pickles RN/RM,
Maternal and Child Health Nurse

Survive and Enjoy Your Baby

GLOBAL
PUBLISHING
G R O U P

Global Publishing Group
Australia • New Zealand • Singapore • America • London

Survive and Enjoy Your Baby

How to Find Your Path to Parenthood

BELINDA JOYCE

Midwife, Maternal and Child Health
Nurse and Mother

First Edition 2017

Copyright © 2017 Belinda Joyce

National Library of Australia

Cataloguing-in-Publication entry:

Creator: Joyce, Belinda, author.

Title: Survive And Enjoy Your Baby : How To Find Your Path To Parenthood / Belinda Joyce.

ISBN: 9781925288698 (paperback)

Subjects: Parenthood.
Infants--Care--Popular works.
Infants--Health and hygiene--Popular works.
Parenting--Handbooks, manuals, etc
Mothers--Life skills guides.
Self-management (Psychology)

Published by Global Publishing Group
PO Box 517 Mt Evelyn, Victoria 3796 Australia
Email info@GlobalPublishingGroup.com.au

For further information about orders:
Phone: +61 3 9739 4686 or Fax +61 3 8648 6871

I dedicate this book to my loving husband Peter and our beautiful children, Jasmine, Mason, Eve and Piper who have brought so much joy to my life and taught me so much.

I also dedicate this to all the families I have worked with over the years and those I am yet to meet.

Acknowledgements

Writing this book has been a major achievement in my life and without the belief, help and support of many it would not have happened.

Firstly, I wish to thank my parents who have always loved me unconditionally and been there to encourage me in everything I do. You have been fantastic role models for me in my own parenting.

My husband Peter who has believed in me and supported me to follow my dreams and encouraged me to write this book. Without our team work this book would never have been completed.

To my amazing children, Jasmine, Mason, Eve and Piper who have been very understanding and positive throughout the book-writing process even though that meant they saw less of me.

To my friends and family, there are too many to name who have helped me to stay on task, supported me throughout and proofread chapters for me, thank you, you made this book so much better.

I thank all the families I have worked with over the years, it has been both an honour and a privilege and I look forward to continuing this work into the future.

To all of my midwifery and maternal and child health nurse colleagues who have taught me so much and have been there for support during challenging times.

I would like to thank my publisher Darren Stephens and his amazing team at Global Publishing Group for making my dream of writing this book a reality and for reminding me to think big and share my message with the world.

FREE
Bonus Gifts

To help you even more I have provided these bonuses valued at over $500:

- *Baby Sleep Flowchart* valued at **$97**

- *Printables* including:
  - Sleep tracker
  - What to put in the nappy bag
  - Hospital bag checklist
  - Childcare bag list
  - Feed tracker
  - Essential equipment for your baby
  - Important contacts list
  - Travel checklist

  ... valued at **$47 each**

- *Tip Sheet For New Parents* worth **$47**

And other tools to help with your new baby.

Claim your free bonuses by going to:

www.BelindaJoyce.com

Contents

Positioning Statement 1

Introduction 3

Chapter 1: Everything you need for your baby 7

Chapter 2: Caring for your baby 29

Chapter 3: How to feed your baby.. 47

Chapter 4: Breastfeeding.. 51

Chapter 5: Bottle feeding 77

Chapter 6: Moving on to solid foods 89

Chapter 7: Crying, sleep and settling...101

Chapter 8: Play and development..125

Chapter 9: Getting out and about with your baby...........................139

Chapter 10: Parents' health and wellbeing 147

Chapter 11: Returning to work..159

About the Author... 169

Recommended Resources... 171

Positioning Statement

Red Nose (formerly SIDS and Kids) vision and purpose is a future where no child dies suddenly and unexpectedly during pregnancy, infancy or childhood, and supporting people impacted by the death of a child.

Our Safe Sleeping Public Health Campaign was launched in 1990, and since that time we have saved the lives of over 9,000 babies and reduced the incidence of SIDS and sleeping accidents by 80%. During this time we have worked with government and state and territory health networks to ensure all new and expectant mothers receive evidence-based information to support them to sleep baby safely and reduce the risk of sudden and unexpected death in infancy.

Belinda Joyce, a maternal and child health nurse, midwife and author of *Survive and Enjoy Your Baby* has broken down some common topics and challenging areas for new parents to help them find their own pathway to parenthood.

We thank Belinda for choosing Red Nose as her charity of choice with 10% of profits being donated to the Red Nose Safe Sleeping campaign.

red
nose
saving little lives

Introduction

Introduction

> *"At every birth, two people are born*
> *– a baby and a mother."*
> **Ancient Indian wisdom**

Congratulations, you're having a baby (or maybe you've already had your baby!). There is nothing else in life that will change your world quite like having a baby, particularly your first. This is going to be the most amazing adventure of your life!

While some planning before the birth is important there is, however, nothing that will prepare you for the all-encompassing sense of wonder and the experiences that having a baby can create, like the strong emotions, both positive and negative, sleep deprivation and the workload your baby will produce. Going through this is all part of the parenting experience – some would say a rite of passage. There will be challenging times as well as many satisfying and enjoyable times. Before having our first baby we thought we would have seven… well that number dropped dramatically after realising the gravity of the decision!

When I see families, particularly mothers, in my work as a midwife and maternal and child health nurse, I see first-hand the pressure that society seems to put on them and, to be honest, I remember it from when I had my first baby. You want to be the best parent possible for your precious new baby and so, for some parents, this may mean they have many plans. Perhaps they want to have a natural birth, to breastfeed and never use a dummy, or even only use natural baby products. Perhaps they want to use organic foods or dress their baby in brand-name clothing, have the nursery made up like in the magazines and get back to their pre-pregnancy weight like celebrity mothers do… many of these unrealistic expectations which we have little control over, make parenting and enjoying your baby more challenging. And not to mention making us feel inadequate as

parents when we can't meet these unreasonable expectations. And I hated that feeling.

Every family is different and what will feel right for one parent may not for another. My philosophy on parenting is simple and family-centred. It allows families to find their own way to parent by giving many safe options to try in a non-judgemental way. Although most new parents would agree they receive too much well-meaning advice, I suggest looking at this as a menu of options – trying some and leaving others.

I truly believe "it takes a village to raise a child" and it is wonderful if you have family and friends close to you to help support you through this new transition into parenting.

Throughout this book I will refer to all carers as parents, and at times will use the term mother and father as well as partner. I hope this does not offend any readers if this does not reflect your family. I acknowledge that there are many different family structures and have cared for, during my many years of experience, traditional nuclear (one mother and one father) families, single mother and single father families, blended families and same sex families. I have also worked with many families where the grandparents or another relative such as an aunt or uncle are the primary carers for a myriad of different reasons. There is no one size fits all approach for a family, and all families have amazing strengths. When I refer to your baby I will alternate between 'she' and 'he'. As I have had babies of both genders and don't want to refer to your baby as an 'it'.

A parent's job description often includes: teacher, chef, nurse, entertainer, cleaner, shopper, coordinator of family duties, the list goes on… it is the most challenging role you will ever take on as it is 24 hours a day, seven days a week and you are emotionally involved in a way you may have never been before.

In Australia, we are fortunate to have child and family health nurses in each state. All have slightly different titles and roles – in Victoria we are

called maternal and child health nurses. We are both registered nurses and midwives with postgraduate qualifications in child and family health.

We provide support and information to families free of charge from birth up until school age. We complete regular health and development checks and support parents with concerns such as feeding, sleep, growth and development as well as parent's own health and wellbeing. First-time parent groups – historically called mothers' groups – are established through these services. Most provide a home visit for the first visit and then further visits are at your local health centre. Research has shown that babies, children and families who attend these visits have better outcomes.

I have written this book to empower more parents and families to feel confident in their very important parenting role and to enjoy their family. By giving safe options to try as well as some personal stories along the way to show that even so-called professionals face challenges.

You are your own baby's expert, not a health professional, no one knows or loves this baby like you.

*You **will** find your own path to survive and enjoy your baby.*

Chapter 1

Everything you need for your baby

Chapter 1

Everything you need for your baby

> *"Try to look at all the advice you get as a new parent as a menu of ideas to choose from and try."*
> **Belinda Joyce**

Having a baby is a wonderful excuse to indulge the shopaholic in all of us and there are some essential items that all families will need. However, much of what you see in baby stores is optional and may not be required, or can be borrowed from friends and family that have had babies themselves or given as gifts from loved ones. Here is a list of a variety of baby equipment and what you should consider before buying them. For those who prefer it, I've added a shopping list at the end of this chapter but I do encourage you read the details before purchasing. Like everything in life, you will find what works best for you over time. Ask friends and family what has worked for them to get tips.

Some stores sell bundles that include a bassinet with matching cot and change table or similar.

This chapter will include:

- Sleep equipment
- Nappy change equipment
- Bathing equipment
- Feeding
- Getting out & about
- Clothing
- Play equipment
- Safety equipment
- Second-hand equipment
- Nursery equipment shopping list

Sleep equipment

- **Cot:** There are many different styles to choose from, so you should be able to find one that suits your tastes and your home. Cots purchased new in Australia should comply with Australian Safety Standards and therefore be safe for your precious baby. It is best to purchase from a reputable retail store – occasionally unsafe cots are sold online, so if buying online, make sure you are familiar with the product and brand.

  Most cots are adjustable with two levels, upper for young babies allowing easy access for parents during those early months, and a lower level for after your baby can sit up. Always ensure the side of the cot is up when baby is in the cot. Some cots have an option to transition into a small toddler bed by removing the sides later.

  If using second-hand, it is best to buy one manufactured after 2003 so it complies with the current safety standard. It is often difficult to know when a cot was manufactured, but if buying from a licensed second-hand dealer there will be a 'compliance plate' stating the year of manufacture. However if buying from a garage sale or online you may not know. It is best to buy from people you know.

  Antique cots, while an attractive piece of furniture and may even be a family heirloom may not adhere to safety standards and increase the risk for your baby to sleep in.

  I recommend two cot sheet sets, cotton blankets and a mattress protector. I can't stress enough the benefit of a mattress protector, it will save your mattress often, and one that can be tumble-dried or two for when one is being laundered is a good idea. Many a night I was glad the mattress had a barrier against a soaked-through nappy. It allowed me to resettle our baby back in her cot once the sheets were changed because the mattress itself was nice and dry.

There is no need for anything else such as pillows, woollen underlays, cot bumpers, wedges or quilts – these may increase the risk for your baby (see the 'Crying, sleep and settling' chapter for safe sleep information). No product has been proven to reduce the risk of sudden infant death syndrome (SIDS), so be cautious about any product that makes this claim.

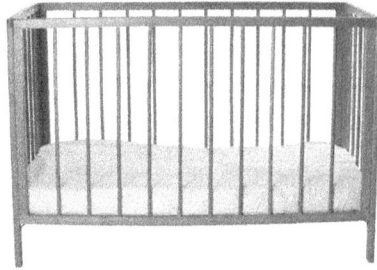

- **Bassinet or cradle:** Not recommended by health professionals and safe sleep experts as they have no mandatory safety standards, therefore experts recommend using a full-size cot from birth.

However in my experience the majority of families still choose to use a bassinet as they are small, able to be moved between rooms and easily fit in the parent's bedroom. If you do choose to use one, please ensure the sides are 300 mm higher than the top of the mattress, that the mattress is firm, fits snuggly and is up to 75 mm thick, that it has good air flow, no hood, and if it has wheels that they are lockable, with no fabric draping down the sides for decoration, no ribbons or trims which could become strangulation risks. And as soon as your baby shows signs of rolling, move them to a cot.

It is not that I am against bassinets for babies, they just require more careful consideration and review. In fact we used a bassinet for our second child as it could fit in our room – our house was very small and the cot was being used by our first child.

Safer bassinet: simple, good air flow, no dangerous decoration.

- **Baby wraps/swaddles/sleeping bags:** To swaddle your baby these are not necessarily essential, however I recommend them, especially for newborn babies as they are used to being confined in mum's tummy, the swaddle or baby wrap can give them a sense of containment and security. It also reduces the startle reflex limiting them waking themselves up.

  100% cotton, cotton jersey or muslin are best, as they breathe well and will not overheat your baby – see safe wrapping tips in the 'Crying, sleep and settling' chapter.

  Swaddle bags are not recommended if they contain the baby's arms or pin the baby into a position – simply using a wrap is much safer.

  As your baby gets older a baby sleeping bag with arms out and movable can be helpful.

- **Folding portable cot:** Portable cots give you some freedom and allow for holidaying while sleeping your baby safely. Even though the mattress is very firm, do not add extra mattresses or bedding to the base as this is a suffocation risk. They are not designed to be used for long-term sleeping, only for occasional use. Very handy for travelling, holidaying, babysitting at other locations than home or even day trips when your baby needs a sleep.

To be sold in Australia these must comply with mandatory safety standards. Make sure you read the instructions, these are also printed on the inside of the cot, often below the mattress. These must not be used once your baby is over 15 kg.

Nappy change equipment

- **Change table and mat:** As you are going to change so many nappies over the first two years of your baby's life, the table is better for your back, although you could use a change mat on the floor if you prefer and certainly for older babies this can be safer when they just keep trying to roll off the table. Look for 100 mm barriers on either side to reduce the chance of falling. Never leave a baby unattended on a change table, it's best to keep one hand on them at all times.

- **Nappies:** Once again there are many choices available. Disposable or cloth – either traditional cloth (flannelette or towelling) squares which you fold or modern cloth nappies which tend to Velcro or clip. Once again this is personal choice based on price, availability, disposal and environmental concerns. A nappy service is another option where the nappies are laundered and returned clean by a company.

In my own experience, I have used both traditional cloth and disposable nappies and I found disposable to be much more convenient although quite expensive. My husband and I felt that despite the cost, the advantages of disposable nappies far outweighed the constant soaking, washing and drying of cloth. Cloth nappies need to be soaked in a nappy bucket in laundry soaker with a tight lid and will be a load of washing a day. I also found my babies in disposable were much less likely to develop nappy rash as the technology keeps the moisture away from baby's skin. There is an environmental impact to consider.

- **Nappy wipes:** Once again many choices, these are convenient for cleaning the baby's bottom during nappy changes but also for so many other jobs including the baby's face, hands, yourself and cleaning up spills. Choosing a fragrance-free type will help reduce chemicals and there are more natural varieties available as well as water only wipes. Swap and change between a few brands to find your favourite type, some are thicker, some thinner and some wetter. A travel pack is handy for in the nappy bag.

Some parents prefer to use a face washer or thin cloth with water, particularly if your baby has a reaction to wipes. Just soak in a nappy soaker and launder as required.

- **Nappy rash barrier cream:** There are many brands on the market, a simple zinc and castor oil based cream works well as a barrier.

Bathing equipment

- **Baby bath:** They will outgrow this quicker than you think but it does make bathing in the early months easier, it can be placed on a kitchen bench, table or in a larger bath. Be careful with emptying this as it can get heavy, removing some of the water with a jug can help take the pressure off your back.

- **Soap free baby wash and shampoo:** Natural unscented bath products tend to be gentler on babies' sensitive skin, there are many different brands on the market, there is no need to spend large amounts of money on this. The huge walls of baby products at the supermarket and department stores can be a little overwhelming, so ask friends and family what they used.

Getting out & about

- **Prams:** There are many different types to choose from. These are covered by mandatory safety standards. It is worth spending a little extra for a lightweight model if possible so that you can lift it in and out of the car with ease.

We started out with a heavy old-fashioned style pram which we loved, but by our fourth baby we found a more user-friendly lightweight and easily collapsible model. It's great if the pram can face toward the parent pushing so they can interact and your baby can feel safe and secure, and later when baby is more interested turn them around to show them the world.

Try to choose a model where the base can be completely flat rather than curved or bent in the middle for your baby's development, and then it can fold up as they grow to a seated position.

Always read the instructions for safe use and use the harness every time baby is in the pram, even when little and unlikely to roll. A five-point safety harness goes over each shoulder, around the waist and up between the legs, keeping baby safe and secure.

All prams come with brakes and a wrist-tether strap, this stops the pram rolling away if distracted – accidents have occurred where prams have rolled away from the control of parents into traffic, onto train lines or into waterways, so get into the habit of using the tether strap.

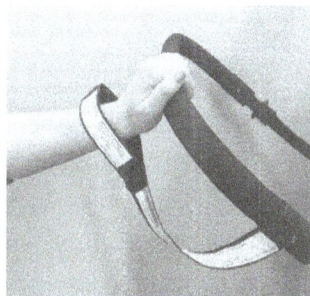

Most prams are fitted with a storage rack underneath, use this for storing your nappy bag as hanging a heavy bag on the handle can sometimes ruin the balance of the pram and flip it over, particularly when removing the baby from the pram – trust me, I have done this.

Prams are not a permanent sleep environment for babies. Your baby should be supervised if they are asleep in a pram and don't cover the pram with a blanket as this can cause overheating.

- **Stroller:** (optional) for later when your baby sits well, these often have less adjustability but are lightweight, smaller in the car and great for travelling. You could keep using your pram, depending on lifestyle, we found a stroller to be quicker and easier.

- **Car restraints:** All new car restraints sold in Australia must comply with mandatory safety standards. It is best to buy new or if buying second-hand it's best to buy from a reliable person or company. If a car seat has ever been in an accident it must be disposed of.

From birth to six months babies must be in a rear facing restraint, and from six months to four years of age must be in either a rear facing restraint or forward facing with inbuilt harness. Check your restraint instructions for more information on when to turn from rear facing to forward facing, this is usually based on weight rather than age.

There are a few choices:

- a capsule type seat that usually suits from birth to six months and can be taken in and out of the car with baby inside. One of the benefits of the capsule style is that some can also fit into your pram. Always place the capsule on the floor or connected to the capsule base in the car or pram before strapping in your baby, avoid placing on a table or couch which may be unsteady.

- a convertible car seat that faces rear to begin with and then moves to forward facing when your baby reaches a certain weight.

There are many different brands and types on the market, ensure you read the instructions for installation and use. It is best to have your car restraint professionally fitted at an approved fitting station, see your local road traffic authority for locations.

Ensure the preferred car seat will fit in your car, it is surprising but some cars which look like family cars don't actually fit a rear facing child car seat.

- **Nappy bag:** If you like to accessorise then there are some great styles to choose from, some look like large handbags and some more unisex. Don't forget it needs to fit nappies, wipes, change mat, extra clothes, a baby wrap, snacks for yourself. Decide on whether you want to use a separate handbag as well or if you will incorporate this into the nappy bag. Pockets can be very handy for this purpose especially for your phone and keys.

- **Baby pouch/carrier:** optional but very handy especially if your baby is unsettled and you are trying to get things done. Follow directions for safe use, ensure your baby's face is visible at all times and not covered by the pouch or pressed against your body. If your baby is unwell, under four months, premature or has a low birth weight use extra caution when using a pouch as there have been deaths especially with those that put baby in a 'C' position with chin to chest, where slow suffocation has occurred. Red Nose do not recommend any soft fabric slings as they do not provide adequate support structure and can add to the risk of suffocation. More structured pouches are fully adjustable as well as better for posture and safety for the wearers back.

Follow the TICKS rules for safe baby-wearing to ensure your baby is safe.

The T.I.C.K.S. Rule for Safe Babywearing
Keep your baby close and keep your baby safe.
When you're wearing a sling or carrier, don't forget the **T.I.C.K.S.**

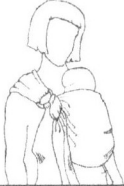

✓ TIGHT
✓ IN VIEW AT ALL TIMES
✓ CLOSE ENOUGH TO KISS
✓ KEEP CHIN OFF THE CHEST
✓ SUPPORTED BACK

TIGHT – slings and carriers should be tight enough to hug your baby close to you as this will be most comfortable for you both. Any slack/loose fabric will allow your baby to slump down in the carrier which can hinder their breathing and pull on your back.

IN VIEW AT ALL TIMES – you should always be able to see your baby's face by simply glancing down. The fabric of a sling or carrier should not close around them so you have to open it to check on them. In a cradle position your baby should face upwards not be turned in towards your body.

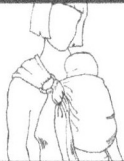

CLOSE ENOUGH TO KISS – your baby's head should be as close to your chin as is comfortable. By tipping your head forward you should be able to kiss your baby on the head or forehead.

KEEP CHIN OFF THE CHEST – a baby should never be curled so their chin is forced onto their chest as this can restrict their breathing. Ensure there is always a space of at least a finger width under your baby's chin.

SUPPORTED BACK – in an upright carry a baby should be held comfortably close to the wearer so their back is supported in its natural position and their tummy and chest are against you. If a sling is too loose they can slump which can partially close their airway. (This can be tested by placing a hand on your baby's back and pressing gently - they should not uncurl or move closer to you.)
A baby in a cradle carry in a pouch or ring sling should be positioned carefully with their bottom in the deepest part so the sling does not fold them in half pressing their chin to their chest.

TICKS used with permission of the UK Sling Consortium.

- **Baby carrier:** optional, goes on your back like a backpack, baby must be at least four to five months of age with good head/neck control. Follow instruction on how to adjust and keep baby securely restrained. Useful for travelling, hiking or going to busy places where there is no space for a pram.

Breastfeeding

- **Nursing bras:** It can be helpful to be fitted for one later in the pregnancy however many department stores now have a great range of maternity bras which you can fit yourself. Practise opening and closing these with one hand as you will be holding your baby in the other hand. It is hard to know which size to buy, maybe just purchase two before the birth and then allow a few weeks after the birth to decide which size and style to buy more of. Most women's breasts enlarge significantly when the milk comes in on day three to five after the birth, but this will settle over the next week or so.

- **Nursing pads:** disposable or cloth to catch any breast milk leakage. Disposable are more absorbent, these can also help to hide nipples showing through clothing. Some women will have very little leakage and some will need these every day.

- **Breastfeeding pillow** or simple triangle shaped pillow; optional but works well to lift baby up to a comfortable height to breastfeed, which improves posture and comfort.

- **Breast pump:** manual or electric, if only using occasionally a manual pump will be all that is required but if returning to work or expressing often an electric model is best. Hospital-grade pumps can be hired, particularly if the baby is in the special care nursery and you are pumping all feeds.

  Be aware that many brands of pump will only connect with the same brand of bottle.

- **Bottles:** If you are wanting to feed the baby a bottle of expressed breast milk or using some formula, you will need a bottle, see below bottles and teats section.

Bottle feeding

- **Bottles and teats:** you will need six bottles with newborn sized teats, these flow slower than teats for older babies. Currently the most popular brands seem to be wide neck bottles with a flatter type teat, trying to mimic a human nipple. None have actually achieved this and therefore a standard shaped teat is fine for most babies and these can be rubber or silicon. Be aware that if you buy a particular brand of bottle, you will most likely require that same brand of teat, trying to stick with a standard size means it will be compatible with many teats and be more useful. Bisphenol A (BPA) free bottles are considered safer and recommended by some experts and health bodies, although BPA is not banned in Australia, it has been linked to some health concerns, look on the packaging to check.

- **Steriliser:** Cleans equipment by removing bacteria. Electric or microwavable are fine, electric is more expensive and stays on the bench and takes up more space where as the microwavable can be stored more easily in a cupboard and is much quicker to use. It is important to follow the directions to ensure the feeding equipment is properly sterilised. You can use a large saucepan and boiling water to sterilise, see the 'Bottle feeding' chapter.

- **Formula**
  - Most standard cow's milk based infant formulas suitable from birth are very similar and unless your baby has a diagnosed medical condition or there are cultural or religious reasons, no particular brand is better than another – paying a higher price does not mean the formula is any better. It must be suitable from birth and most brands call this a Stage 1 or Step 1 formula and these

have all the nourishment needed for a newborn baby. A formula with a lower protein level is preferred as it will be closer to protein levels in breastmilk, high protein formula has been associated with overweight and obesity in later life.

· All infant formula sold in Australia and New Zealand, that is suitable from birth to 12 months of age, and is regulated by the food standards code, is safe for your baby.

See the 'Bottle Feeding' chapter for further details.

- **Cleaning equipment**
  · Bottle and teat brushes for washing.

Feeding your baby solid food

- **Highchair:** you won't need this right away but it is an essential item to help with the introduction of solid foods. A highchair can be useful to place a baby in while you work in the kitchen and around living spaces. It helps them sit up and engage with the environment. It must have a five-point harness so that your baby can't climb or slip out. Once again many different types are available, including free-standing options, and add on to chairs (booster) options. If possible, choosing one that reclines a little is handy as a younger baby can start to use it from an earlier age.

- **Mat for under highchair:** Can also be handy but is not essential on non-carpeted areas that are easy to clean, however it would be advisable to choose one that is at least one metre square to protect the floor from spills.

You can buy plastic tablecloths by the metre from fabric stores and there are a great range children's designs with car tracks etc., which can be used for play later.

- **Bowls, plates, utensils:** Again, not needed until at least four to six months. Many to choose from, plastic is best and use utensils with no sharp edges.

Clothing

- **Baby clothing:** is often the most fun and like any clothing is obviously seasonal and you can liken to your own personal style. However personal flair aside there are some practical options. The basics are often a staple ensemble of most infants.

  Practical choices include:

  - All in one jumpsuits; make sure the button or zip is at the front for ease of changing nappies, particularly overnight.
  - Think ease of laundering, no ironing required.
  - Natural fibres breathe better.

  Because clothing choices are personal, I will not give you a full list but consider:

  - at least five singlets.
  - five day outfits which may be all in one and used for night also.
  - a few cardigans or jumpers.
  - some bibs, quick release style with Velcro or snap fasteners, no ties or strings – remove before sleep time.
  - some hats, especially if winter.

  No need to buy too many as you will soon see which works best for you and your baby, and remember you may receive many gifts from family and friends, generally in newborn sizes. Also your baby will grow quickly and these first outfits will not be worn for long. It always amazes me how quickly newborns grow. All of our children began growing out of their smallest clothes within the first few weeks of life. Family and

friends may give you their baby's second-hand clothes and because they have not been worn for long they are usually in great condition, I think this is the best kind of recycling. And it is always pleasing to see other children and families getting a similar enjoyment and experiences in the garments your own children have worn and grown in.

Accessories for play

- **Hanging mobile** for interest and infant engagement, it can sometimes be musical, maybe placed above change area, some can attach onto side of cots but, for safety it is better to fix to the ceiling instead.

- **Play/activity gym** that your baby can lie under and look at toys and eventually learn to touch hanging toys. Encourages early development depth perception and hand-eye coordination. It also encourages using multiple hemispheres of the brain.

- **Toys** suitable from birth to 36-month old children: must comply with mandatory safety standards, this ensures there are no small pieces which may fall off and become choking hazards, and that they are durable even when dropped on a hard surface. These are often toys such as rattles, large shapes for sorting, balls, figurines, blocks, stuffed toys, push along and ride-on toys.

  I know it sounds like common sense but it is easy to overlook the packaging and the suitable age for a particular toy. I remember my husband wanting to purchase all sorts of toys marked as suitable for three years and over for our babies, most times I think he wanted to play with it more than our children!

- **Books:** any are good, however board or fabric style are ideal for babies, black and white with high contrast pictures are enjoyed by young babies. The melodic sound of a parent reading is both soothing and reassuring for little babies and little books can be taken anywhere chewed on and played with.

- **Playpens:** Another non-essential item but can be very handy, these are most useful once baby can move around the house, rolling or crawling. You can place baby inside and know that they are in a safe place while you are cooking, going to the toilet or saving the world from a toddler invasion. It must be sturdy with sides at least 500 mm high and bars 50–95 mm apart to avoid trapping baby's head.

- **Bouncer/rockers:** Not essential but can be a place for your baby to see what is going on and you can move it around the house or outside. Ensure it has a crotch strap so baby can't slide out the bottom, and a stable base with rubber tips to prevent movement when baby rocks. I found these great for taking baby around the house with me, outside to hang out washing or into the bathroom so I could shower. Never place this on a table as it may fall.

- **Baby walker:** Not required or recommended and many accidents have occurred in these devices mainly because of the wheels falling down steps, and encouraging babies to walk before they are ready can negatively affect development. A stationary play centre is a safer option which is similar without the wheels but once again not required.

- **Push along:** a toy that a baby can stand behind and push along. These need to be heavy enough so that the baby does not pull it over. These offer stability for an adventurous and active baby or toddler as they find their confidence and develop body balance.

Other

- **Safety gates:** Are very useful for keeping a mobile baby out of dangerous areas such as the kitchen or near stairs both top and bottom. Avoid gates with a fixed bar at the bottom which creates a tripping hazard.

- **Baby monitor:** There are many types of monitors available including audio-only, breathing (apnoea) monitors and some with cameras also. While I am reluctant to suggest that certain monitors are unnecessary it all comes down to choice. I feel that breathing monitors can sometimes cause stress to parents as they alarm when babies take a slightly longer pause in breathing or when baby moves into a different position. While monitors can provide some peace of mind, there is no evidence that they reduce the risk SIDS or fatal sleep accidents. Those with a camera may be helpful to be able to see what your baby is doing but not necessary.

A simple audio-only baby monitor gives you the freedom to move around the house or even to go outside and know your baby is not crying. I found this great for hanging out the washing or doing some gardening.

If there is a specific medical reason for your baby to be monitored your paediatrician will discuss this with you.

Please do not hang or attach any monitor to your baby's cot, place it on a piece of furniture nearby.

- **Baby thermometer:** Digital works well for times of illness, these are small and inexpensive, just get placed under baby's arm and can verify that your baby either has or has not got a temperature. There are many different types available that can go in the ear or over the forehead but these are not necessary for normal home use.

- **Infant nail scissors or clippers:** Your choice but be careful, I have seen the skin of many fingers accidently trimmed rather than nail. It is often easier to clip them when baby is asleep or while feeding.

- **Soft baby hairbrush:** This can be a good tool to gently exfoliate the scalp and reduce the chances of cradle cap.

- **Safety equipment:** Such as cupboard and fridge locks which are great for in the kitchen, furniture corner protectors, electrical socket plugs and door slam protectors are all useful, especially once your baby is on the go.

  Smoke alarms should be in every home but on this list as a reminder to check they are in good working order.

Second-hand product tips

Second-hand products are a great place to start, good for the budget and the environment.

Questions to ask yourself:

- Is the product clean with no broken parts?
- If it is a cot, does the mattress fit well?
- Are there any missing pieces such as safety harnesses?
- If a car restraint, has it ever been involved in an accident?
- Are the instructions available?

If the product is more than five years old do not purchase.

If buying from a garage sale or online, no laws protect you and no Australian standards labelling is required.

It is safer to buy second-hand if you know the seller.

Some items available to purchase for your baby may be unsafe, currently there are mandatory safety standards for: cots, folding portable cots, prams and strollers, dummies, toys for babies and toddlers, baby bath aids, baby walkers, children's nightwear and car restraints. This means many items have never been tested, always ask yourself if products appear safe.

If you find something that may be unsafe, please report this to the ACCC Phone 1300 302 502 or productsafety.gov.au

Nursery Equipment Shopping List

Sleep equipment:

- ☐ Cot and mattress
- ☐ Cot sheet set x 2
- ☐ Cotton blankets x 2
- ☐ Mattress protector x 2
- ☐ Baby wraps, cotton or muslin x 4 or more
- ☐ Portable cot, optional

Nappy change equipment:

- ☐ Change table and mat
- ☐ Nappies: fabric squares/modern fabric/disposable newborn size
- ☐ Nappy wipes: large and travel size pack
- ☐ Nappy cream: barrier cream zinc and castor oil type

Bathing equipment:

- ☐ Baby bath
- ☐ Soap free baby wash
- ☐ Baby shampoo

Getting out and about:

- ☐ Pram
- ☐ Car restraint: suitable from newborn
- ☐ Nappy bag
- ☐ Baby sling, optional

Chapter 1: Everything you need for your baby

Breastfeeding:

☐ Nursing bras

☐ Nursing pads: disposable or washable

☐ Breastfeeding or triangle pillow

☐ Breast pump: if expressing

☐ Bottles: for expressed milk if required

Bottle feeding:

☐ Bottles x 6

☐ Teats x 6 newborn size

☐ Formula suitable from newborn

☐ Steriliser: electric or microwave

☐ Cleaning equipment: bottle and teat brush

Feeding solids:

☐ Highchair

☐ Bowls, plates, utensils

☐ Mat for under highchair

Clothing:

Based on personal choice, consider:

☐ at least five singlets

☐ five day outfits which may be all in one and used for night also

☐ a few cardigans or jumpers

☐ some bibs

☐ some hats, especially if winter

☐ booties, socks and mittens

Play accessories:

- ☐ Hanging mobile
- ☐ Play/activity gym with hanging toys
- ☐ Rocker/bouncer
- ☐ Toys
- ☐ Books
- ☐ Playpen

Other:

- ☐ Safety gate if needed
- ☐ Baby monitor
- ☐ Baby thermometer digital type
- ☐ Infant nail clippers/scissors
- ☐ Soft baby brush

Chapter 2

Caring for your baby

Chapter 2

Caring for your baby

> *"Your greatest contribution to the universe may not be something you do, but someone you raise."*
> **Unknown**

How to care for your newborn baby

Your confidence in caring for your new baby may depend on how familiar you are with babies – have you been around many babies, did you have younger siblings that you helped care for, have you baby-sat for friends or family? Because we were one of the first of our friends to have a baby, we both had limited experience with routine tasks such as nappy changing, bathing, and handling a young baby, and I see many parents who feel the same way. I had always loved babies and would be the first in line to have a cuddle, but I had never been left alone with a young baby and when they cried I had always given them back to their mother.

I have seen other parents who have had a lot of experience caring for friends and family's babies before having their own and therefore they knew how to do many of these tasks with confidence.

Regardless of your level of expertise or confidence with handling babies, all new parents will learn to care for their babies even if they feel overwhelmed to begin with. While there are many online resources available there are also many people to ask for support including midwives, friends, family, child health nurses and your doctor.

How to change a nappy: You will change many nappies every day, most parents will learn this skill while in hospital with help from their midwife. There are no big rules here, as long as the nappy stays on and is not too tight it will be fine.

For a dirty nappy, wipe any poo away with the front of the nappy and then use some wipes or a wet cloth to clean the bottom area.

With girls always wipe from front to back to avoid pushing poo toward the vagina. Even if you can see poo in the vagina, just gently wipe over the top and the rest will come out on the next nappy, this also helps to avoid giving your baby thrush.

With boys just wipe over the penis and scrotum area, if your son is uncircumcised there is no need to pull back his foreskin to clean it as it is attached to the penis and cannot move at this age.

Be alert, as just removing the nappy can make your baby wee, this is more dangerous with boys! A quote from my husband, "Holster his weapon".

When changing a disposable nappy try to have the tabs at the back so they will fasten at the front, most parents have tried it the other way and it is more difficult. If using traditional cloth nappies, you can find many different ways to fold these for different sized babies.

Using a nappy cream can help to avoid nappy rash, some babies need this more than others, it can be applied in a thick coating when required.

Bathing: Most babies dislike their first few baths – I think they feel frightened as they are naked, unwrapped and often cold. Newborn babies are used to being secure in their mother's uterus all warm and snug, so having their limbs out can make them feel vulnerable. Try placing an extra face washer over her chest and tummy and keep her warm. As soon as the water starts to cool down, get her out and dry her as quickly as possible.

You don't have to bath your baby every day as you will be cleaning her bottom every nappy change. Maybe just a clean of face and hands with a

warm wet face washer each day. Some parents and babies enjoy bathing daily and that is fine.

Bathing can be done at any time of day, some babies get stimulated by the bath and others get drowsy, if this is the case maybe a bedtime ritual of bathing would work well. Many partners enjoy bathing their baby, so evening may work well for this.

Keep the water temperature between 37–38 degrees Celsius, any hotter and scalding can occur, cooler can drop baby's body temperature. You can get bath thermometers to help or test the water temperature on your own arm.

Bathing should be fun, no rules are needed, as long as your baby's face stays above the water she will be able to breathe. If you cradle your baby with an arm running under her shoulders and upper back and link your pointer finger and thumb around her upper arm, her face can't slip under the water. As you practise bathing you will become more confident and even start to turn her onto her tummy occasionally over your arm with her chin supported by your hand. Most babies come to enjoy bath-time, floating in the warm water, arms outstretched and free.

As in the nappy changing section, your baby's genitals only need a gently wipe over with a wet washer in the bath.

Even when your baby is older and sitting well, never leave her alone in the bath as she may slip and drown. If you need to answer a phone or the door, take her with you wrapped in a towel.

As she gets older you will need to move to the big bath and expect lots of kicking and getting wet. Bath-time will become playtime and can be a good activity when your baby is unsettled, unwell or overtired.

Common newborn concerns

First few days after birth: Don't be shocked if your newborn baby looks a little different than you expected, often she will have a cone-shaped head from the forces exerted through the birth process, this will usually 'round out' over the first few days of life. Many babies have some swelling and redness to the face and eyes which will gradually improve. Depending on type of birth this may be worse if forceps or vacuum have been used to assist with the birth, again this will heal quickly.

Umbilical cord: The umbilical cord will be clamped and will dry over the first few days, try to keep it out of the nappy if possible. There is no special treatment, just keep it dry, after bathing dry in and around the cord stump gently with a cotton tip. Usually this will fall off in the first ten days. If the skin around it becomes red and it is smelly see your doctor to check it is not infected.

Sticky eyes: This is a very common newborn problem due to blocked tear ducts. Unless the white of the eye is red it is not conjunctivitis and simple treatment at home will usually help. Using either saline, cooled boiled water or expressed breastmilk on a clean cotton ball, wipe the affected eye from the inside to the outside in one sweep then discard that ball and start with another. If the eye is stuck closed use more liquid to soak it open. It is important to use a clean ball each 'sweep' of the eye to remove the bacteria.

The tear ducts will usually open and begin to drain well within the first few months of life. If it remains a problem up to 12 months of age a small procedure to open the tear duct manually can be performed. Talk to your child health nurse, doctor, or paediatrician about this.

If the white of the eye is red and inflamed and there is a lot of green pus, see your doctor as this may now be conjunctivitis and require antibiotic eye drops to treat.

Birthmarks: Some babies have birthmarks at birth or they can develop soon after birth, there are a number of different types so ask your midwife, child health nurse or doctor to explain what type it is and if it is a permanent or will fade over time.

Swollen chest/breast area: This occurs in many newborn babies, even boys and will usually reduce gradually over the few weeks after birth, this is caused by the mother's hormones circulating in your baby. Sometimes there is even some milk leaking from them, don't be concerned it will go away with no treatment.

Jaundice: Very common in newborn babies, jaundice causes babies skin and the whites of the eyes to become yellow, it normally spreads from the head down the body, the further down the higher the level and the baby is more likely to require treatment. Good frequent feeding in the first few days of life reduces the risk of jaundice, premature babies are more at risk. Jaundice levels are tested by taking a heel prick blood sample to test the level and treatment is usually in hospital with light therapy. Most jaundice does not require treatment and the skin colour will be normal by two weeks of age, but occasionally this persists.

Baby acne/hormonal rash: This is a pimple-like rash to the face, neck and sometimes upper chest and back. Almost half of all babies will experience this by around six weeks of age, usually around the time you are having professional photos taken! Experts are still unsure of the reason for these but mother's hormones in the baby's system are thought to be involved, perhaps her skin being exposed to the air and bacteria for the first time may also play a part. There is no treatment for this, do not squeeze the pimples/spots, just wash them with clean water and do not use soap. If they become dry as they heal, apply a moisturiser such as sorbolene or a natural variety. After having beautiful clear skin at birth this change in appearance can be upsetting for many parents but only time will improve this.

Chapter 2: Caring for your baby

Cradle cap: Is a form of dry skin on the scalp, caused by the sebaceous glands. First it becomes a little dry, then crusty and begins to form a cap over the baby's scalp. Moisturising is important, sunflower oil works well, as it has a natural mild acidity that helps break it down. It is also important to gently exfoliate the scalp to prevent the build-up of dry skin in the bath when the skin is soft and wet, rub a washer back and forth gently on your baby's head. You can use a soft baby brush on a dry scalp also. Occasionally the dry crusts form in the eye brows, be particularly careful close to the eyes but use the same treatment.

All of my babies had some degree of cradle cap and it can look awful, I can remember putting a hat on them whenever we went out until it improved.

If persisting you can try a medicated preparation from the pharmacy and if this fails see your doctor or paediatrician, occasionally a baby will be very badly affected and require expert advice and treatment.

Dry Skin: Many babies get dry skin, some are even born with it, particularly if they were overdue. First look at the bath products you are using, do they contain sodium lauryl sulphates – these are cheap foaming agents and are well known to dry the skin and cause dermatitis and eczema. Try moving to a more natural product that does not contain this. Bath oils can be helpful. When bathing, gently exfoliate the dry flaky skin with a wet washer.

Moisturise, moisturise, moisturise. There are many products available, a simple sorbolene cream often works well, there are products available specifically for babies with dry skin as well as many natural varieties. You can moisturise your baby many times a day – when you're changing nappies is a good time and your baby will probably enjoy it too. If your baby still has dry skin, see your GP or paediatrician.

Reflux: Many babies suffer from reflux, where the muscle at the top of her stomach does not hold tight enough to keep the milk down so she vomits often. More frequent, smaller feeds may help. If formula feeding,

changing formula brands often makes no difference, using a slower teat may assist.

As long as it is not creating pain and she is gaining adequate weight it is not usually a problem requiring treatment, however some babies vomit so much that they don't gain enough weight or the constant vomiting causes pain, crying, difficulty breathing or coughing. See your doctor or paediatrician if you think your baby may benefit from medication to reduce reflux.

AR (anti-reflux) formula can help to keep the milk down, however more research is needed in this area. If using AR formula, never make this up early for a feed as it tends to set like concrete in the bottle, it must be made freshly for each feed.

Colic: This is abdominal pain where the baby draws her knees up to her chest and cries for long periods of time. There are many different theories regarding colic but none proven and many conflicting descriptions about what colic is. In the medical world, it is often defined as a baby that cries more than three hours a day, for more than three days a week for more than three weeks, although there is no scientific evidence to support this. Colic is not a serious medical issue and most babies who suffer from it have no underlying illness.

The experts believe that in the western world, about 25% of all babies suffer from this condition. Colic appears as severe abdominal pain possibly caused by trapped wind. Many believe it is caused by gut immaturity. This crying usually peaks at around six weeks of age and for many baby's this prolonged crying has greatly improved or stopped by 12 weeks of age. The baby appears otherwise healthy and well, if in doubt see your doctor or paediatrician and ask for a thorough examination to rule out any medical cause.

You could try massaging her tummy in a clockwise direction and cycling her legs to help her pass wind or do a poo. Changing formula if you are formula feeding may help but don't change too often. Some formulas

contain probiotics which may improve colic symptoms although more research is needed. You could try some over the counter wind or colic medications available from the chemist – there is no strong evidence to show these help but many parents find them very helpful and if you follow the directions on the label they are believed to be safe.

When your baby gets sick

There will be times when your baby becomes unwell and you will want a medical opinion and some advice on their care. Parents are their own baby's experts, you know her better than anyone and if you feel something is wrong it is worth seeing a doctor, if it is not urgent, you should start with your general practitioner (GP). If after seeing a doctor you don't feel any better, ask for a second opinion or go to another clinic. Don't ever feel that you are overreacting or being an inconvenience, your baby is precious and you have every right to seek support.

Seek urgent medical help if your baby:

- Has difficulty breathing or rapid breathing.
- Is vomiting up most feeds or not taking feeds.
- Has less than five heavy wet nappies in 24 hours.
- Is limp, lethargic or floppy.
- Has a red or purple coloured rash or a rash that when gently pressed does not fade.
- Has a stiff neck.
- Has pale or blueish skin.
- Has a seizure or fit.
- Has a temperature over 38 degrees Celsius.
- Has diarrhoea that is not improving.

Medical help

- If serious call 000 and ask for an ambulance.
- Go to your local emergency department.
- If less serious see your doctor if within clinic hours.
- After hours, you can try the National Home Doctor Service for in home, bulk-billed visits, call 13SICK (13 74 25).

Coughs and colds: All babies tend to suffer many cold viruses in their first year of life, these range from just a runny nose and mild cough, to becoming very unwell and needing to see a GP or paediatrician. For many babies the biggest problem is the blocked or snuffly nose, as babies are nose breathers, and it makes feeding and sleeping very difficult if her nose is blocked. If breastfeeding you can try to squirt some breastmilk up her nose, or drip it up. Another option is to try some saline drops, available from the pharmacy, these help her to sneeze and clear out his nasal passages. Using the drops or breastmilk before a feed will help her to feed more comfortably, she may need shorter more frequent feeds. Some babies are fussy or refuse breast or bottle feeds when they have a cold sometimes, due to a sore throat or just feeling miserable, and the difficulty is that he is unable to tell you. Just keep trying. If over six months of age, don't be surprised if she refuses food for the same reason, continue on with breast or bottle feeds and offer some cool boiled water in a sipper cup.

Most colds get better with no treatment required apart from some extra cuddles and attention. If your baby is miserable and you think she is in pain or has a high fever you could give infant paracetamol, make sure to follow directions on the bottle and don't use for longer than 48 hours unless under medical care. Avoid using aspirin as well as cough and cold medications as they are not safe for this age group.

Occasionally what appears to be a simple cold virus may turn into a more serious infection such as a chest infection, croup, ear infection, bronchiolitis or pneumonia. If your baby is not getting better and is unwell, in pain, not feeding well, has a temperature, see your doctor or paediatrician, antibiotics or other treatment may be required.

Fever: A temperature above 38 degrees Celsius is considered a fever and it is usually a sign that your baby's body is fighting an infection. Try to keep your baby comfortable by using less clothing and bedding – a tepid or lukewarm (not cold) bath can be comforting. Give frequent small feeds and if formula fed, try small amounts of cooled boiled water.

The raised temperature is the body's way of trying to fight the infection so only use paracetamol or other medications if she is irritable and miserable. If your baby is less than three months of age, seek medical care early with a fever, to rule out more serious causes.

Diarrhoea and vomiting: Gastroenteritis or 'gastro' as it is commonly named, is usually highly contagious and will often effect full households – wash your hands many times or use some antibacterial hand gel. If your baby usually vomits, you will be able to tell the difference as the vomit is usually much more in quantity and smells offensive. The diarrhoea is usually very offensive in odour. Most times the vomiting will pass within one or two days, but the diarrhoea may take longer; the greatest risk is dehydration.

Most babies will want to feed less, if breastfeeding, then more frequent and smaller feeds work well. If bottle feeding, give small amounts of water often for the first 12 hours and then normal strength formula, starting with small amounts and gradually increasing to normal, as tolerated by your baby. Your baby may benefit from rehydration solution, you can discuss this with your doctor or pharmacist. If your baby is over six months he may or may not want food, as long as he is having adequate fluids he will be fine. Doctors now believe that there is no reason to restrict food, you can give your baby any food he wants to eat as tolerated.

See your doctor if not improving as babies can deteriorate quickly.

Dehydration signs: a sunken fontanelle on top of his head, sunken eyes, loose pale skin, small concentrated urine, cold hands and feet or difficult to wake. Immediate medical care is required.

Occasionally the diarrhoea could be a sign of food intolerance, allergy or caused by antibiotics or other medications. Discuss this with your doctor.

Thrush: White spots or patches in the mouth, on the tongue, on gums or inside the cheeks, appearance of cottage cheese. Her mouth may be sore and feeding may be reduced, refusing the breast, detaching on and off from the breast.

Treat the baby's mouth with an antifungal oral gel (miconazole) this can be obtained over the counter from pharmacies. It must be applied safely, by measuring the suggested quantity of gel and placing it on a clean finger and rubbing on baby's tongue, roof of mouth and inside cheeks, do not use the supplied spoon in baby's mouth or leave a 'blob' of the gel in your baby's mouth as this could be a choking hazard. Use the gel as directed for one week and continue treatment once a day for a further one to two weeks to reduce the chance of recurrence.

Nystatin oral drops can be used but are much less effective at treating oral thrush. Use as directed, again continue treatment once a day for a further one to two weeks to reduce the chance of recurrence.

Sterilise all feeding equipment well and replace dummies weekly if possible.

Often a bright red spotty nappy rash also develops, treat with an antifungal cream as directed.

Mother: nipples may be pinker than usual and more tender. Many women describe shooting or burning breast pain after feeds and between feeds. Apply antifungal cream or oral gel in a thin layer to both nipples after each feed during the day, for at least a week, no need to wash off the oral gel before feeds. Keep nipples dry by changing breast pads as required.

Teething: Most babies get their first teeth between six and twelve months of age, although occasionally a baby is born with a tooth or they begin erupting early, whilst others have none until 12 months of age. The central two bottom teeth are the most common first teeth and then the upper central teeth next, although your baby can get them in any order. Most children will have all 20 baby teeth by three years of age.

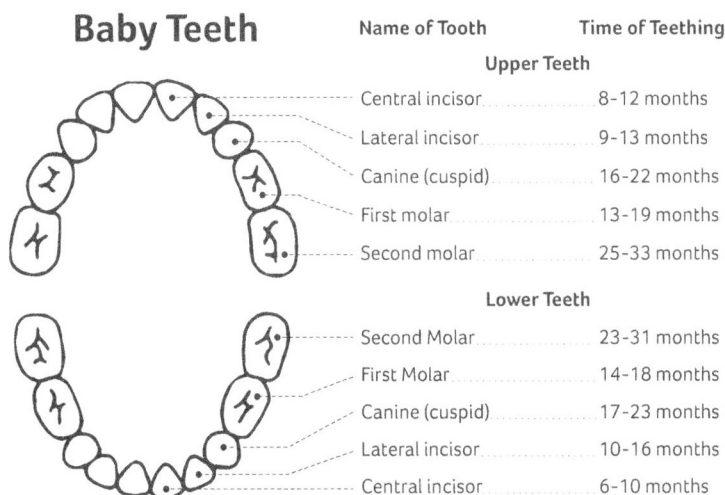

Baby Teeth

Name of Tooth	Time of Teething
Upper Teeth	
Central incisor	8-12 months
Lateral incisor	9-13 months
Canine (cuspid)	16-22 months
First molar	13-19 months
Second molar	25-33 months
Lower Teeth	
Second Molar	23-31 months
First Molar	14-18 months
Canine (cuspid)	17-23 months
Lateral incisor	10-16 months
Central incisor	6-10 months

For some babies this is a painless process, but for many there is some pain associated with teeth cutting through the gum. Signs and symptoms of teething are red cheeks, dribbling, biting his own fists, biting your nipple or bottle teats, pulling at his ears, nappy rash, refusing feeds/solids. These symptoms can come and go for many months with no teeth erupting and can disrupt sleep patterns in the process.

You can try rubbing your baby's gums gently with a clean finger – this seems to help and they will often have a bite on your finger at the same time. There are many different teething toys, some of which can be placed in the fridge to become cold and then given to your baby to chew on. A wet face washer placed in the fridge can also be relieving for your baby to chew on when their gums are inflamed.

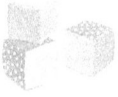

Some parents find over the counter teething medications helpful as well as paracetamol and ibuprofen – follow directions carefully and these should not be used every day for long periods. Teething gels can help but remember they are still a drug so always follow the direction on the tube.

Some babies develop fever and illness when teething, this is not caused by teething but more from their immune system being lower due to the teething. See your doctor if your baby appears very unwell.

Constipation: This is when your baby's poo becomes hard and dry, and passing a poo is painful – sometimes they can even get small tears around the anus from passing large, hard poos. It is normal for your baby to go red in the face and spend some time pushing on and off before passing a poo, but they are only truly constipated when the poo is firm and dry, often in small pieces like rabbit droppings.

Breast fed babies rarely become constipated and there is a large variance in what is normal, they often pass many poos a day as a newborn and then they slow down. Some breastfed babies can go up to two weeks between poos and still not be constipated.

If moving from breast to bottle feeding you will probably notice your baby's poos becoming firmer and passing them less frequently, this is normal.

If your baby is constipated try:

- Gentle massage in a clockwise motion on his abdomen and cycle his legs

- Check formula is being made up correctly

- Add an extra 10 ml of water to the bottle or offer small amounts of cooled boiled water for a week

- Change formula, try a 100% whey based formula

- Discuss with a health professional, child health nurse, doctor or paediatrician.

Cow's milk protein allergy: Normal cow's milk based formula will be difficult for these babies to digest and so we see symptoms such as: vomiting, diarrhoea, hives, anaphylaxis, and wheezing. If diagnosed, an extensively hydrolysed formula will need to be prescribed for these babies. Be guided by your doctor or paediatrician, often these babies will grow out of this problem and be able to tolerate dairy as they get older.

Medications

Paracetamol: Reduces pain and fever. If your baby is miserable and you think she is in pain or has a fever you could give paracetamol, make sure to follow the directions on the bottle and don't use for longer than 48 hours unless under medical care. I found the brands that had a 'suspension' form of paracetamol, which is a thicker syrup type liquid, were easier for my babies to swallow rather than being thin like water.

Ibuprofen: Reduces pain and fever, alternative to paracetamol. Only use over three months of age and after feeding.

Cough and cold medications: avoid use in under six year olds.

Antibiotics: can only treat bacterial infections and must be prescribed by a doctor, use as directed by your doctor.

Avoid using aspirin, cough and cold medications as they are not safe for this age group.

It is safest to only give medications under the advice of a pharmacist or doctor.

Immunisation

By immunising your baby on time, they will have the most protection available against infectious diseases such as measles, mumps, rubella, diphtheria, tetanus, whooping cough, polio and hepatitis. In Australia, immunisations are free and available from immunisation nurses and doctors at your local council and GP clinics. Unfortunately, some of these diseases have been increasingly reported throughout Australia in recent years. Some government payments are linked to immunisation.

Vaccines go through rigorous testing to ensure safety, there is often pain and redness at the injection site, but these types of reaction usually resolve quickly.

If you want more information on childhood immunisations including diseases, safety of vaccines and myths about immunisation:

http://www.immunise.health.gov.au/

Summary

- Over the first year of life your baby will be exposed to many illnesses and will pick some up and avoid others. This is how your baby's immune system develops.

- Handwashing reduces the spread of illnesses.

- Keep immunisations up to date.

- Consider attending a basic first aid course, some courses are aimed at parents of babies.

- Find a good family doctor that you feel you can trust, this may require visiting a few different doctors.

- Find a paediatrician if your baby has ongoing medical concerns

- Remember you are your baby's expert, so if you are concerned about your baby's health get a second opinion or ask for a referral to a Paediatrician who specialises in the care of babies, children and adolescents.

Chapter 3

How to feed your baby

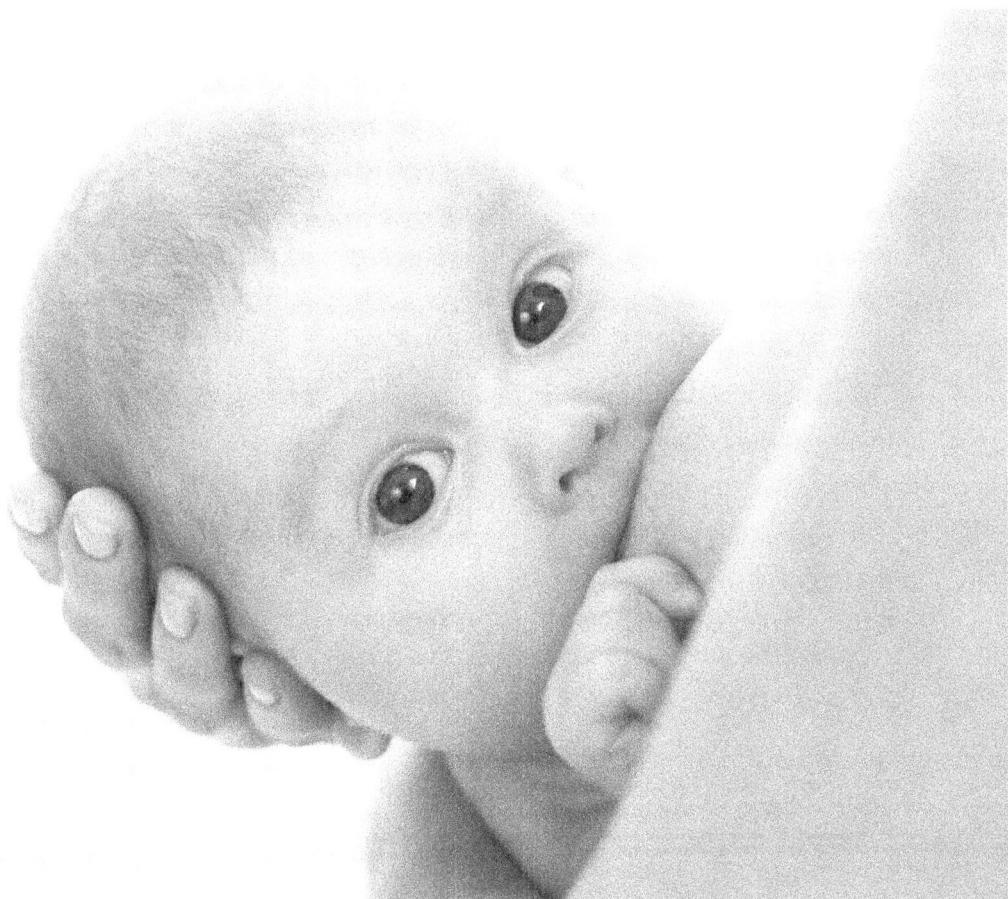

Chapter 3

How to feed your baby

> "A new baby is like the beginning of all things –
> wonder, hope, a dream of possibilities."
> **Eda J LeShan, writer, counsellor, educator**

How to feed your baby

There are a variety of influencing factors that impact on the decision of whether to breast or bottle feed your baby. Expectations forced on us by friends, family, media, society and then our biggest critic, ourselves. Parents, and particularly mothers, have hopes, dreams, fears and anxiety – how do I want to feed my baby, will I be able to breastfeed, do I want to breastfeed, will people judge me if I choose to bottle feed my baby?

The choice of how to feed your baby is a very personal one and one that should be an informed decision.

Breastfeeding is the natural way to feed your baby and for many mothers it is very important to them to successfully breastfeed their baby. It is reassuring to know that most women will be able to successfully breastfeed, given good support and information. There has been much research done in the last 20 years which has greatly improved the ability of health professionals to assist women to successfully breastfeed.

All research studies and other sources of information show that breastfeeding is by far the best and healthiest choice for your baby, however for some women and families breastfeeding is not successful

or not best for them and they decide not to continue, reasons include: medical conditions for mother or baby, medications not safe to use while breastfeeding, low milk supply, pain and damage to nipples not improving with support, not feeling comfortable breastfeeding, work commitments, unsuccessful with breastfeeding their last baby and many other reasons. And for many mothers the decision to bottle feed can be made worse by feelings of failure and self-doubt because, for whatever reason breastfeeding didn't work out for them and their baby.

Others choose to bottle feed with formula from the beginning for many of the same reasons above. Sometimes these mothers feel judged or misunderstood by the midwives at the hospital or even their own friends and family about this decision.

Many mothers choose to combine both breastfeeding and bottle feeding with formula for a variety of reasons including low milk supply, work commitments, wanting more freedom, or a partner wants to help bottle feed their baby to reduce the mother's workload and expressing is not the preferred option.

Please read the breastfeeding and bottle feeding chapters for more detailed information on each feeding method. But know that I will not judge you for your decision, I want to support you with which ever method you choose.

Chapter 4

Breastfeeding

Chapter 4

Breastfeeding

> *"I think all parents are just trying to do the best for their children."*
> **Belinda Joyce**

Breastfeeding

For help deciding how to feed your baby, see the 'How to feed your baby' chapter.

This chapter will look at how to get started and answer some common questions mothers ask about breastfeeding, as well as discussing some common challenges. There are entire books written on breastfeeding and this chapter does not have the scope to discuss all situations. If you are facing breastfeeding challenges please look at the resources section at the end of this chapter for support and assistance options.

There is no special preparation required for your breasts, your body does this itself during your pregnancy. Perhaps just getting used to handling your breasts a little more, as this will become common after the birth. Try to avoid using soaps on the breasts as they can lead to drying of the breast and nipple. Avoid bras with underwire during your pregnancy and during breastfeeding as these may also affect your milk ducts and lead to blockages.

Some prenatal education on breastfeeding either in classes, with a midwife or lactation consultant, is helpful but not essential. Reading this chapter will be a good starting place.

Chapter 4: Breastfeeding

Benefits of breastfeeding:

- Breastmilk is a complete meal for your baby, no other food is required until around six months of age.
- Contains omega-3 long-chain fatty acids DHA important for brain development.
- Breastmilk is easily digested.
- Less illness as breastmilk contains antibodies which protect your baby from ear and respiratory tract infections and gastroenteritis.
- Lower risk of heart disease as an adult.
- Reduced dental decay.
- Lower risk of sudden infant death syndrome (SIDS).
- Breastfeeding is important in the development of mouth and jaw as well as vision and speech.
- Your baby's digestive system is lined with all the correct good bacteria.
- Less likely to develop allergies or type 1 diabetes.
- Close bonding time with skin to skin contact, gives baby comfort and stimulates hormones beneficial to breastfeeding.
- Once established it is quick and gets quicker over time.
- Free and portable.
- Environmentally sustainable.
- No preparation of formula required.

For mother:

- Mothers uterus contracts and reduces in size more quickly, less bleeding.
- Mothers weight reduces as extra calories are used for making milk.

- Mothers have lower rates of osteoporosis, cervical cancer, breast cancer, heart disease, osteoporosis and type 2 diabetes.

- Delays fertility for mother is exclusively breastfeeding.

- Mother gets a chance to stop and rest while breastfeeding.

And many more…

Positioning and attachment

Good positioning and attachment are the keys to successful and comfortable breastfeeding.

When your baby is in the correct position attached to the breast your nipple will not be damaged and she will stay attached longer as milk removal is easy and she will stay active there.

No matter what position you are in the principles remain the same:

1. Make yourself comfortable, perhaps supported with a cushion in your lower back and if required you can use a pillow, triangle pillows work well to bring baby a little higher, just below nipple line is good.

2. Move your baby towards you, so that you can stay in a comfortable position, after all you may stay there for a long time.

3. Baby unwrapped, close to your body, face, chest and hips all in alignment facing your body. Hold her back and shoulders rather than her head if possible.

4. Try to align your baby's nose with your nipple and have her head slightly tilted back, bringing her chin towards the breast helps to keep her nose free to breathe.

5. 'Tease' baby to open her mouth wide by rubbing the nipple from her nose to lips, when baby has a wide, open mouth, bring her toward you and point the nipple towards the roof of her mouth.

6. Baby's lower jaw needs to take a large mouthful of the breast, most of the areola (darker area around the nipple) will disappear under the baby's lower lip but some will probably still be visible above the baby's upper lip and this is fine.

7. You should see and feel strong rhythmical sucking with some pauses and hear swallowing of milk.

8. Allow your baby to breastfeed as long as she wants if you are comfortable.

9. When she finishes give her a short burp by holding her upright against you and giving her back a gentle rub and pat. This need not take long and if she does not burp that is okay.

10. Offer her the other breast in the same way, she may or may not want this. Most babies will need both breasts for a full feed but as a newborn and depending on supply they can sometimes only take one side.

11. If you want to break the attachment for any reason, always put your little finger into the corner of baby's mouth first, this avoids damaging the nipple.

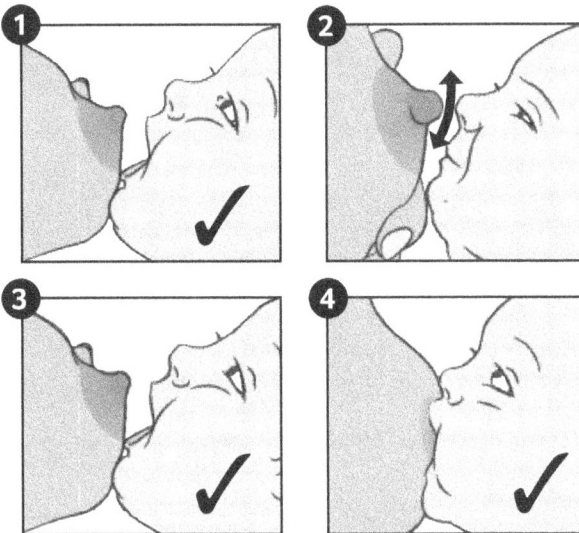

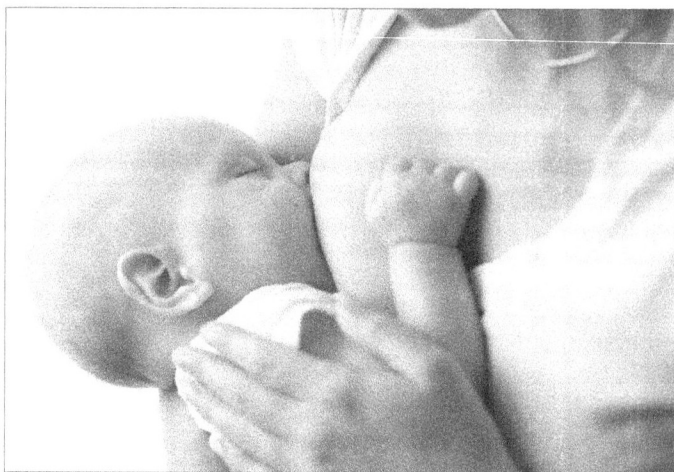

Good attachment, chin to breast, nose clear

Lips flanged open

Common breastfeeding positions

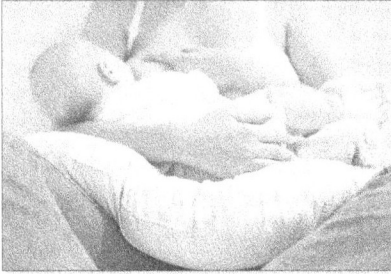

Cradle hold

Transitional hold

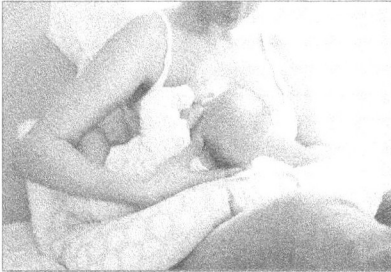

Football hold

Side Lying

How to begin, the first breastfeed

This is a very special time and as long as your baby is full term and breathing well the first breastfeed will usually occur within the first hour or two after birth. If your baby is held skin to skin with her mother and not taken away for weighing and measuring, then most will instinctively start to search for the nipple, sometimes a small 'froth' of saliva bubbles appear around their mouth and they poke their tongue in and out. It is best not to disturb this special time with hospital procedures like weighing, unless medically required. You can use your baby's instinctive behaviours and reflexes to help initiate and establish breastfeeding well. You can move her closer to the nipple but try to allow her to find the nipple herself. Using the above positioning and attachment ideas try to attach baby to the breast. Allow her to suck for as long as she wants to as long as it is comfortable, when she comes off offer her the other breast.

If a baby is placed on her mother's tummy soon after birth, skin to skin, she will eventually crawl up to the breast and attach herself to breastfeed. There are many videos of this available online, just search 'breast crawl', it is amazing. The full crawl is not necessary however allowing the baby to find the nipple herself is part of allowing her instincts to work as they should. Researchers have found that many of the newborn's primitive reflexes that had been thought to be unnecessary actually help your baby to search for the breast and nipple as well as to breastfeed.

Although breastfeeding is the natural way to feed your baby that does not mean you will know how to do it – it is important to have some support from your midwife or birth attendant to ensure this first breastfeed goes well. As discussed it is best to allow your baby to find the nipple herself however sometimes some help is required especially if mum is very tired from the birth or had a caesarean birth and finding it difficult to change position.

The first week of breastfeeding

During the first week of breastfeeding there will be many changes as your baby's needs change and the amount of milk available changes. At birth the breast produces small amounts of colostrum, a thick yellow liquid, high in sugar, fat, protein and antibodies.

On the first day of life, a baby will only get around ½ teaspoon of colostrum from both breasts put together each feed, this quantity matches the small stomach size she will have.

On the second day, one teaspoon and from them on the milk volume increases rapidly. These small breastfeeds are digested quickly, so frequent feeding is common and necessary.

In these early days, most babies will want to feed from both breasts as the quantity is so small. Babies are born with extra fluid on board to cope with these first few days of small amounts of breastmilk and colostrum, they actually lose up to 10% of their birth weight over the first three to four days and this is normal. Their stomachs are very small and will stretch over time, see diagram below.

Newborn Baby Stomach Capacity

DAY 1

Size of a cherry
5 - 7 ml / 1/2 tsp

DAY 3

Size of a walnut
22 - 27 ml

1 WEEK

Size of a plum
45 - 60 ml

1 MONTH

Size of a large egg
80 - 150 ml

The more breastfeeds your baby has in the first few days the more milk supply you will have over the next few months. It is best to breastfeed your baby before they start to cry as crying is a late hunger sign. An early feeding cue is the rooting or searching reflex: turning her head side to side with a big wide open mouth and putting her hand/s in her mouth. If breastfeeding is initiated before crying, your baby will probably attach better and feed for longer. Less crying means less stress for both parents and baby. If you are in hospital, having your baby in your room usually results in many more frequent breastfeeds, less weight loss, better milk supply and more stools from your baby and reduces the chance of significant jaundice.

If your newborn baby is very sleepy and not waking for at least eight to twelve breastfeeds during each 24 hours then you may need to wake her and feed her, and ask for support and advice. The saying 'never wake a sleeping baby' does not apply during the first few days or weeks, until your baby is breastfeeding well and gaining adequate weight.

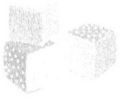

	urine passed	stools (poos) passed
Day 1	1	1 black meconium
Day 2	2	2 black meconium
Day 3	3	3 black/greenish
Day 4	4	3–4 green/yellowish
Day 5	5+	5+

More urine being passed is better but less is concerning, talk to your midwife or doctor. After day four we expect a minimum of five heavy wet nappies every 24 hours.

The first few stools passed are black, thick, sticky meconium, the substance that has lined the digestive system for some months. It is important to pass meconium during the first days of life to reduce the chance of your baby becoming jaundiced. The more stools passed the better, the table above is minimum requirements. Colostrum has a laxative effect so if she is breastfeeding well usually meconium will be passed early. By day three or four this meconium will become transitional, meaning some milk is coming through and it becomes more green, and by day five most stools are a soft mustard yellow colour. Stools that turn green or yellow sooner just mean your baby is feeding very well. Newborn stools can look watery, seedy, curd like, vary in colour from yellow to green and usually have no offensive smell.

Newborns do not usually breastfeed at regular intervals, they have periods of the day when they are more unsettled, more hungry and require more frequent breastfeeds. It is important to allow them access to the breast when they want to breastfeed, this is called demand feeding.

Once your milk has 'come in' which usually means a large over supply of milk for a few days and feeling like your breasts don't quite belong to you! Your baby may have larger stretches between breastfeeds or she may demand feeds more frequently because she is getting mostly foremilk which is the equivalent to a big drink of water with very little fat content to sustain her. If this is the case try to allow your baby to fully empty the first breast before offering the second, this way they first receive the lower fat content foremilk and then the higher fat hindmilk from the first breast, this enables good weight gain and growth. When you are very full this may mean she only takes one breast each feed for a few days or weeks and that is fine. If your other breast is uncomfortably full you can express for comfort or use a breast shell, milk collection cup that fits over your nipple to collect the dripping milk. You can use this expressed milk in future for other feeding opportunities, perhaps your partner would benefit from the bonding experience of feeding their baby from a bottle while mum has a well-deserved sleep.

Weight gain

This very much depends on your baby, their birth weight, genetics and any medical conditions that they may have.

In the early days, it is normal for your baby to lose up to 10% of their birthweight in the first week but we aim for them to have regained this by two weeks of age or three weeks at the latest.

Early weight checks should be at least 48 hours apart to avoid unnecessarily alarming parents as the baby could appear to have lost weight due to the weight check being before or after a feed, baby passing urine or having a large bowel movement prior to weighing. Something as trivial as a discrepancy between two different scales used to measure your baby's weight can add undue stress and worry for no reason. If this may have occurred, try to use the same scales for future weight checks.

No weight gain or loss of weight over a few days must be taken seriously and an assessment of breastfeeding technique by your midwife, lactation consultant or maternal and child health nurse is required. If breastfeeding appears to be going well but weight gain remains low then a thorough medical examination is required to exclude medical illness.

The best way to monitor growth over time is by using a growth chart, in Australia the World Health Organisation (WHO) growth charts are usually

used and we expect babies to grow in a similar curve to that on the graph. If a baby seems to be crossing growth curves particularly downward, an assessment of feeding and a medical examination is required.

Average weight gain	
Birth to 3 months	150–200 gms a week
3 to 6 months	100–150 gms a week
6-12 months	70–90 gms a week

Don't be alarmed if your baby is not gaining exactly this amount, be guided by your health care professional and if you are worried get a second opinion.

I feel that there is often too much emphasis put on weight gain and there is a large variation of what is normal in growth and if your health care professional is not concerned then you shouldn't be either.

Watching your baby grow when you are breastfeeding is a very satisfying experience, you should feel proud of yourself and your baby for getting it right.

Feeding length and frequency

Breastfeeds should not be timed as some newborn babies may suck effectively for 20–40 minutes or more each feed with some pauses between and others may feed for only ten minutes. If your baby is sleepy during a feed a nappy change between sides can be useful.

Young babies tend to breastfeed around eight to twelve times each 24 hours, this is every two to four hours – be guided by your baby, this is called demand feeding, sometimes she will feed more often and perhaps have a growth spurt or be more thirsty when it is hot.

Early on it can be helpful to keep track of how many breastfeeds, wet and dirty nappies your baby is having every 24 hours as these are often difficult to remember when you are sleep deprived and your midwife,

maternal and child health nurse or doctor will probably ask. You can simply write it down in a note book or there are free apps for your smart phone. Once all is going well feel free to stop doing this.

Cluster feeds

Many newborn babies cluster feed in the evening, they can be on and off the breast for hours and then often have a longer sleep after this. You may find this cluster feeding is repeated every evening at the same time and if this is the case you can try to work around it by organising evening routines such as cooking dinner earlier, don't expect to get anything done at this time of day, remember this won't last forever and in actual fact it is a special time for you and your baby to spend together.

Some mothers can store large amounts of milk and others store less which may mean their babies need to feed more frequently. Regardless of what well-meaning friends and family as well as some popular baby care books state, there is no requirement to stretch out breastfeeds. If your baby is growing well and breastfeeding is comfortable and you are happy then breastfeeding on demand is best. Even we as adults eat and drink at different intervals each day depending on thirst and hunger, so do our babies. The milk received by babies who breastfeed more often and from breasts with a lower supply actually get milk with a higher fat content, which is great for growth. If your baby is feeding too frequently and you want to change it, seeing a lactation consultant may be useful, she will check your positioning and attachment to maximise efficient removal of breastmilk and other troubleshooting.

Expressing and storing breastmilk

Many mothers will need to express breastmilk within the first few months of breastfeeding, some reasons include: full breasts, mastitis, baby admitted to special care nursery, mother baby separation, returning to work, increasing supply, allowing mother to skip a feed overnight and rest while partner feeds baby. On weekends my husband would often give our first baby a bottle of expressed milk in the middle of the night allowing me more rest time which made a big difference and he really enjoyed doing it.

There are three methods of expressing: by hand, manual hand pump and electric pump. The choice of method will depend on how often you are needing to express, time available, cost and availability. Electric breast pumps are quicker and usually remove more milk than manual, hospital-grade is best if you have a baby in special care nursery requiring all feeds expressed. Ask a midwife to show you how to hand express before you leave the hospital if possible.

When expressing always wash your hands first, set yourself up with a glass of water, baby close by to look at or a photo as just looking at your baby will help with removal of more breastmilk quicker. A private, quiet, warm room, a warm shower before expressing can help.

How to express by hand

1. Wash hands well with warm water to help warm your hands.

2. Massage the breast with gentle strokes towards the nipple, roll your nipple a little between your fingers, this helps to trigger the let-down reflex.

3. Use a clean dish to collect the milk, hold under the breast.

4. Use thumb and finger on the edge of the areola (darkened area around the nipple) to press inwards and squeeze together.

5. Repeat this process in a rhythmic way, you may feel the milk ducts under your finger.

6. When milk flow almost stops, move fingers around to express a different section of the breast and repeat the process.

7. Repeat as above on the other breast.

8. You can swap back and forth between breasts to obtain more milk, if not enough, wait an hour and try again.

9. Pour milk into a storage container such as a bottle and place in fridge.

How to express with a manual hand pump

There are different types of hand pumps available, many are low cost, make sure to follow the directions for use. Second-hand manual pumps are fine to use, if the directions have been lost you can usually find them online, make sure you wash the pump well with warm soapy water and sterilise it before using.

Your breast pump does not need to be sterilised, if you are expressing for a healthy full-term baby at home. If your baby is unwell, ask your health professional for advice. The rules for cleaning and storage of your pump differ depending how often it is being used, if using multiple time a day you can store it in the fridge in a closed container or bag between expressions, if only using a few times a day, rinse milk off with clean cold water and store in a closed container. All expressing equipment should be thoroughly cleaned every 24 hours, take pump apart and rinse milk off in cold water, then wash with warm soapy water using a bottle and teat brush and rinse twice with hot water to remove all detergent residue. Allow to drain upside down on a clean cloth or paper towel and store in a closed container or bag when dry.

1. Wash hands.

2. Massage the breast with gentle strokes towards the nipple, roll your nipple a little between your fingers, this helps to trigger the let-down reflex.

3. Centre pump over nipple.

4. Depending on style of pump use plunger action or squeeze handle gently in a rhythmic action as comfortable.

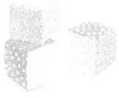

5. When milk flow reduces and breast becomes softer repeat on the other breast.

6. You can swap back and forth between breasts to obtain more milk, if not enough wait an hour and try again.

7. Pour milk into a storage container such as a bottle and place in fridge.

How to express with an electric pump

These can be bought or hired and if returning to work or expressing all feeds for your baby this is the most efficient option.

1. Wash hands.

2. Massage the breast with gentle strokes towards the nipple, roll your nipple a little between your fingers, this helps to trigger the let-down reflex.

3. Centre pump over nipple.

4. Start on low suction and increase as comfortable.

5. When milk flow reduces and breast becomes softer repeat on other breast

6. You can swap back and forth between breasts to obtain more milk, if not enough wait an hour and try again.

7. Double pumping both breasts at once may increase milk supply and saves time.

8. Pour milk into a storage container such as a bottle and place in fridge.

The amount expressed is not the same amount that your baby will receive from a breastfeed, your baby is much more efficient at milk removal, some women find expressing difficult even though their baby is thriving on breastfeeding only.

Home Storage of Breastmilk

Expressed breastmilk should be stored in a sealed glass or plastic container or milk storage bag in either the fridge or freezer. Freshly expressed milk should be cooled in own container before adding to cold or frozen milk. Date containers and freeze any milk not likely to be used within two days. Use fresh expressed milk if available.

Length of time breast milk can be stored

Breast milk status	Storage at room temperature (26°C or lower)	Storage in refrigerator (5°C or lower)	Storage in freezer
Freshly expressed into sterile container	6–8 hours If refrigeration is available store milk there	No more than 72 hours Store at back, where it is coldest	2 weeks in freezer compartment inside refrigerator (−15°C) 3 months in freezer section of refrigerator with separate door (−18°C) 6–12 months in deep freeze (−20°C)*
Previously frozen (thawed)	4 hours or less – that is, the next feeding	24 hours	Do not refreeze
Thawed outside refrigerator in warm water	For completion of feeding	4 hours or until next feeding	Do not refreeze
Infant has begun feeding	Only for completion of feeding Discard after feed	Discard	Discard

*Chest or upright manual defrost deep freezer that is opened infrequently and maintains ideal temperature.

Source: National Health and Medical Research Council

Transporting breastmilk

- Use an insulated container for transport with freezer bricks to maintain temperature.

- Never refreeze thawed or partially thawed milk.

- On arrival store breastmilk in the fridge or freezer if remains frozen.

Using expressed breastmilk

If the milk has been stored in the fridge, stand the bottle in a container or jug of hot water, not boiling, swirl the milk around in the bottle regularly to heat it through. Test the warmth by dripping some milk onto your inner wrist, it should feel warm not hot, overheating breastmilk can destroy some nutrients and scald your baby. Never use a microwave to reheat breastmilk as it creates hot spots and continues heating for many minutes after microwaving.

If the milk is frozen and you have time, allow it to gradually defrost in the fridge. If you need the milk more quickly you can place the sealed container into a bowl of warm water until it thaws, swirl it around to thaw it all, you may need to change the water a few times as it cools down. Only store defrosted milk in the fridge for up to four hours.

Because expressed breastmilk is like liquid gold, do not freeze or defrost in large quantities this is to avoid wastage. A handy trick is to put expressed milk into ice cube trays then you can thaw out and use small amounts without wasting any breast milk and it defrosts faster also.

Breastfeeding challenges

Nipple pain or trauma

Breastfeeding should not be painful, if it is causing more discomfort than nipple tenderness as well as trauma to the nipple, expert help is required from a lactation consultant.

Nipple pain and trauma is often related to a shallow latch where the nipple is compressed against the hard palate and often misshapen after a feed. This can be made more difficult if the breast is engorged or the mother has inverted nipples. It is important to get some support from a qualified Lactation Consultant, many free clinics operate from public hospitals around Australia as well as community and private lactation services.

Go back to the principles of positioning and attachment and try again, try skin to skin contact and allowing the baby to find the nipple herself, allowing the instinctive behaviours to assist.

If breastfeeding is very painful and the nipples damaged, sometimes it is best to remove the baby from the breast for 24 hours to allow the nipple to heal. This requires expressing and feeding the baby the expressed breastmilk in another way such as bottle, cup or syringe. It is best to have support with doing this safely and maintaining milk supply as well as reintroducing the baby to the breast to reduce the chances of severe damage again.

Always break the suction with a finger before removing baby from the breast, their suction is very strong, this alone can damage the nipple.

Some women find a purified lanolin product or hydrogel breast pads can aide with nipple healing and help improve discomfort.

Not enough milk

This is one of the most common reasons for quitting breastfeeding, please get some expert advice if you are thinking of quitting as sometimes there is plenty of milk.

If your baby is not attaching well the milk supply is often lower as they are not stimulating the supply in the same way and they are not removing as much milk as their sucking is less efficient. They may want to feed all the time but then fall asleep after only a few minutes of feeding. These baby's often gain weight more slowly.

Milk supply may be slow to 'come in' if your baby has not breastfed frequently in the first few days of life.

The best way to make more milk is to breastfeed more often or to express, this will increase production. Switch breastfeeding going from one side to the other and then back to the first side and second again. Offering your baby a breastfeed every time he shows any signs of hunger, hands to mouth, rooting/searching reflex.

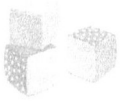

If expressing use a hospital-grade electric pump, these are usually hired, this is much stronger and more efficient as well as quicker. You can also try double pumping.

There are some herbs such as fenugreek which can boost milk supply as well as some medications, these should all be discussed with your doctor as they can interact with other medications including over the counter medications.

Be assured that even if some formula supplementation is required, breastfeeding can continue.

Too much milk

This can be overwhelming for your baby if it flows quickly, gulping and choking while feeding is common as well as excessive weight gain and vomiting, sometimes projectile after feeds.

You can try limiting each breastfeed to one side only, postural breastfeeding by lying back or side lying, which reduces gravity and slows the flow. You could also express some milk off before putting your baby to the breast.

If you have a large supply and you leak from one breast when feeding form the other you can use a breast shell, soft silicon milk collection cup that fits over your nipple to collect the dripping milk. Use breast pads, either washable or disposable to stop leakage. Keep a spare t-shirt in the nappy bags for times of leakage.

Engorgement

This is when the breasts become very full, hot, firm and painful. It is not just milk in the breast but also blood supply and other tissue fluids creating the full breasts, this is often worsened by IV fluids often used in labour. Engorgement used to be considered a normal part of early breastfeeding but we now know it can be avoided by breastfeeding more frequently and fully emptying the breasts once perhaps with a pump.

It makes the breast so firm that the areola stretches and flattens making a deep latch almost impossible. To latch your baby you will need to express some milk to soften the areola area before attempting to latch your baby. This may require only a few hand expressions or a few minutes of expressing.

Feed your baby frequently, even every 1.5–2 hours to allow your breasts to soften. If your baby is not attaching well and breastfeeding, it is important to use a hospital grade breast pump to express and empty your breasts well.

Warm compresses such as a warm wet face washer or cloth before feeds help milk flow and cold packs after or between feeds reduce inflammation, always cover the cold pack with a cloth.

Mastitis

Mastitis is inflammation of the breast which can go from a small tender lump in the breast usually caused by a blocked duct all the way to a full-blown fever with flu like symptoms and excruciating pain. These symptoms can come on very rapidly and without warning.

Breastfeed as frequently as possible, always starting with the affected breast first. Warm cloths and gentle massage before breastfeeds can help.

Wear loose comfortable clothing, bras without wires or seams that could compress the breast tissue. Rest as much as possible and ask for help if required.

Try to determine and correct the cause: tight bra, breasts too full (baby started sleeping through the night or family gatherings where baby went longer between feeds than usual), tired and run down, cracked nipples.

You may require antibiotics if not improving or you are very unwell see a doctor.

Nipple or breast thrush

Baby may have white patches on tongue and inside cheeks, similar to cottage cheese, a thin white coating is normal. Nappy rash may be present that typically has small bright red spots.

Burning or shooting nipple pain, often not associated with feeds. Often the nipples become a brighter pink but sometimes the breasts look no different, they may be itchy. Often this is after initial nipple tenderness has settled. Even if there is no obvious thrush in baby's mouth this is still worth treating for the mothers comfort and to stop it developing in baby's mouth. You both need to be treated otherwise it may continue.

Treatment for mother: a thin amount of antifungal gel or cream to the nipples, continue to apply to the nipples for at least seven days. The oral gel does not need to be washed off before breastfeeding. Change breast pads often if moist.

Treatment for baby: miconazole oral gel is the most effective treatment however careful and safe application is important. With clean hands, measure the correct amount of gel onto the spoon provided but do not use the spoon to put into baby's mouth, use a clean finger and thinly spread the gel on baby's tongue, roof of mouth and inside cheeks. It is important not to give this to your baby in a large 'blob' which could cause difficulty breathing or suffocation. Use this 4 times a day for a week then once a day for another week to reduce the chance of the thrush recurring. Some pharmacists will not supply this gel for use with young babies, if having difficulty, speak with the pharmacist and let them know that you understand how to give this to your baby safely. Your pharmacist may suggest Nystatin drops but be aware these are much less effective.

Wash and sterilise dummies and teats well and often.

If nipple/breast thrush is recurring see your doctor, lactation consultant or child health nurse. You can also look at your diet and reduce or eliminate sugar and yeast as these can make it worse.

Breastfeeding and alcohol

It is safest not to drink alcohol and breastfeed, particularly during the first month while establishing breastfeeding. After one month no more than two standard drinks is recommended, depending on mother's weight and what percentage of alcohol is consumed, two standard drinks will take approximately three to four hours to be cleared from the breastmilk. If you are wanting to drink some alcohol consider expressing breastmilk before to be used until the alcohol is cleared.

Deciding when to stop breastfeeding

The recommendation in Australia is to breastfeed until 12 months and longer if it feels right for you and your baby.

The best way to stop breastfeeding is to do so gradually by dropping one breastfeed every few days and letting your breasts get used to producing less milk. Often the last breastfeed that is dropped is the morning feed as your breasts will be at their fullest and often the feed may be for your comfort until milk production reduces. You risk mastitis and engorgement if you stop breastfeeding suddenly.

If your baby is less than six months old, each breastfeed dropped will need to be replaced with infant formula, be guided by the requirements on the formula can based on your baby's age. If your baby is over six months of age and taking some solid foods you may not need to replace all feeds, be guided by the formula can directions and your child and family health nurse, doctor or paediatrician. See bottle feeding chapter for more information.

Occasionally a baby may refuse the breast before the mother feels ready. This can be difficult for the mother if she does not feel ready to stop. Keep trying at the breast each feed and if refused give expressed breast milk from a bottle. You will need to express regularly to keep your supply if you want to continue giving only breastmilk. Some babies will refuse feeds if they have a sore throat, this should improve as the pain reduces.

Other times you will never find out why they are refusing the breast. You will need to make a decision based on the importance of continuing to breastfeed to you. If you don't want to continue to express and bottle feed you will need to introduce infant formula, gradually is best so that your baby's stomach gets used to this change. See the bottle feeding chapter for more information.

Other breastfeeding considerations

- If taking any medications, herbs or vitamins both prescribed and over the counter, ask your doctor or pharmacist if they are safe to use while breastfeeding. Avoid all other recreational drugs.

- If you consume highly caffeinated drinks such as coffee, tea, cola and energy drinks, try to limit these as these also pass to your baby and can cause irritability.

- If drinking alcohol only drink small amounts as it passes into the breastmilk. Try to wait up to two hours before breastfeeding after drinking. Remember a glass of wine at home is usually much larger than a standard drink from a bar. If planning a big night out, have some expressed milk available or supplement with formula.

- If you are a smoker consider giving up. There are many different strategies, if you have tried before it is worth having another go as it often takes a few attempts before succeeding. Try to smoke outside and use a smoking jacket that can be removed when you go inside and wash your hands, this reduces the chemicals your baby is exposed to. Call Quitline 13 78 48 for assistance.

- In Australia you are able to breastfeed anywhere, it is against the law for anyone to ask you to stop breastfeeding or to leave a restaurant. However early on you may prefer to breastfeed in a quiet private place and many shopping centres have good baby care rooms for this purpose.

- Clothing designed for breastfeeding can be helpful for both comfort and modesty. Some women find that layering with a top that can be pulled up and a singlet that can be pulled down covers their stomach.

Remember if breastfeeding is important to you and you have good support available you will most likely be successful with breastfeeding.

Breastfeeding help

- Australian Breastfeeding Association Mum to Mum help line 1800 686 268

- Your child and family health nurse or the Maternal & Child Health Line 13 22 29

- Your Midwife or Lactation Consultant

- Your own GP or Obstetrician

- GP helpline 1800 022 222

Breastfeeding and medications enquiries

National:	Medicines Line	1300 MEDICINE (1300 633 424)
Victoria:	Royal Women's Hospital Medicines Information Centre	03 8345 3190
	Monash Medical Centre Drug Information Centre	03 9594 2361
ACT:	Medicines Information Services	02 6244 3333
NSW:	Medicines Information Centre	02 8382 2136
	Mothersafe (medications in pregnancy and lactation)	02 9382 6538 (Sydney metropolitan) 02 1800 647 848 (non-metropolitan NSW)
NT:	Medicines Information Services	08 8922 8424

QLD:	Queensland Medicines Advice and Information Service (QMAIS)	07 3646 7599 or 07 3646 7098
SA:	Obstetric and Paediatric Information Service	08 8161 7222
TAS:	Medicines Information Services	03 6222 8737
WA:	Obstetric Medicines Information Service	08 6458 2723

Websites

- www.breastfeeding.asn.au
- www.raisingchildren.net.au
- www.eatforhealth.gov.au
- www.rch.org.au
- www.thewomens.org.au
- www.wslhd.health.nsw.gov.au/Westmead-Hospital
- www.schn.health.nsw.gov.au/
- www.seslhd.health.nsw.gov.au/rhw/

Chapter 5

Bottle feeding

Chapter 5

Bottle feeding

> *"Try to not let your concerns about what other people might think influence the decisions you make for your child"*
> **Jo Frost, Supernanny**

Bottle feeding

- See equipment chapter for list of requirements.

- See 'How to feed your baby' chapter for help to decide on breast or bottle.

Which formula is right for my baby?

The choice of formula is a difficult one for many new parents, I can still remember looking at that large wall of different infant formulas and wondering which was the best for my baby.

Things to consider:

- All infant formula sold in Australia and New Zealand that is suitable from birth to 12 months of age is regulated by the food standards code which means all are safe to feed your baby. This code covers nutrient composition, food safety requirements and food additives.

- Most standard cow's milk based infant formulas suitable from birth are very similar and unless your baby has a diagnosed medical condition or there are cultural or religious reasons, no particular brand is better than another and paying a higher price does not necessarily mean the formula is any better.

- The formula must be suitable from birth and most brands call this a Stage 1 formula and these have all the nourishment needed for a newborn baby until around six months of age.

- Formula with a lower protein level is preferred as it will be closer to protein levels in breastmilk, high protein formula has been associated with overweight and obesity in later life.

- The decision of whether to spend extra money on a 'gold' formula is also difficult, these formulas tend to have extras such as long chain fatty acids added which claim to enhance brain development however there is currently no strong evidence to prove this. If you do choose a 'gold' formula it is good to know that they do not seem to cause any harm.

- Experts agree that cow's milk based formula is preferred rather than goats milk, soy based or modified lactose varieties.

- There is currently no evidence that organic formula is better than standard.

- The use of special formula such as HA type to prevent allergy is not recommended and more research is needed in this area.

- Diagnosed cow's milk protein allergy requires a medical diagnosis and prescription only, 'extensively hydrolysed formula'. Many infants with cow's milk allergy are also allergic to goat's milk and soy milks therefore these are not recommended.

- So far there is not enough evidence to encourage the use of probiotics or prebiotics to reduce allergy.

- Homemade infant formula is not recommended and many recipes suggest ingredients that are thought to be high risk to babies whose immune systems are not fully developed.

- There are a range of infant formulas on the Australian market which claim to treat minor conditions such as colic, constipation and reflux, there is at this stage no evidence that these are better for your

---

baby, and I would encourage you to talk to your nurse, doctor or paediatrician before changing to one of these.

- Infant formula is modelled on breastmilk but it cannot replicate the ingredients and nature of breastmilk, any claim that it can is misleading.

Stage 1, 2, 3

Most formula brands have a 'Stage 1' formula marketed for up to six months then a 'follow-on' or 'Stage 2' formula marketed to six to twelve month old babies, however there is no evidence that changing formula from those suitable from birth is required. The formula marketed to those over six months generally have more iron, protein and some other nutrients however these extra requirements should be gained through a broad diet of solid foods including meat, green leafy vegetables and legumes rather than from formula, in fact the risk is that they may have too much iron. If your baby is growing and developing well, stay on the first stage of formula, it has all the nutritional requirements until 12 months of age. Stage 2 and 3 (toddler) formulas are not required for your baby.

Bottle preparation

1. Wash hands with warm soapy water and use a clean area.

2. Try to make up only one bottle at a time as needed.

3. Ensure bottle and teat have been sterilised, see sterilising section.

4. Boil fresh tap water with a kettle or in a saucepan on stove, allow to cool for 30 minutes until lukewarm, this ensures the boiling water does not destroy vitamins and nutrients in the formula and reduces the risk of scalding. If your baby needs the feed sooner, the sealed bottle of boiled water can be immersed into a container of cold water.

Chapter 5: Bottle feeding

Formula preparation

1. Check formula can instructions on how much water to how many scoops of formula, this is often different between brands.

2. Add exact amount of water to the bottle.

3. Add exact amount of level scoops of formula, some cans have a levelling section on rim of can or use the back of a sterilised knife, tap the scoop on rim of the can to remove air bubbles.

4. Do not change dilution of formula by using half scoops or more or less water, this can lead to constipation, slow weight gain and other problems.

5. Store the scoop inside the can to keep it clean, no washing needed. Only use the scoop supplied with the formula as they can be different between brands.

6. Replace the teat and cap and shake the bottle vigorously so the powder dissolves.

How to safely prepare formula in advance

Formula is best made up at the time of a feed however if necessary it can be made up in advance – follow these steps.

Store the bottles of made-up formula in a fridge at less than five degrees Celsius (41 degrees Fahrenheit) and always use within 24 hours. To warm, immerse sealed bottle in a container of warm water until it has reached desired warmth.

Another way is to store the boiled water in sterilised bottles in the fridge. When needed warm the water by immersing the sealed bottle in warm water and then add the scoops of formula.

Never use a microwave to heat formula as it heats unevenly and can create hot spots and burn your baby's mouth.

How to transport feeds

- It is best to transport the boiled water in sterilised bottles rather than made up formula, refrigerate the water to less the five degrees Celsius before leaving and transport in a cold bag with ice packs.

- There are small containers available for transporting formula powder in, make sure these are sterilized regularly.

- If the formula must be transported 'made up' make sure it has been refrigerated for some time before leaving and transported in a cold bag with ice packs.

- If the trip takes less than two hours the formula can be placed in a fridge at the destination and used within 24 hours, if the trip takes longer it is best to discard any made up and unused bottles and make fresh formula.

How to sterilise

Sterilising removes all bacteria from feeding equipment and reduces the chances of your baby getting sick. There are a number of different sterilising options. Boiling is the preferred option as it gives more consistent results, however an electric or microwave unit is more convenient. The electric unit is large and usually stays out on the bench, whereas the microwave unit can be more easily stored. Chemical sterilising is a less popular method and you should follow the instructions provided with this method.

Boiling

- Wash bottles, teats, caps and other feeding equipment in warm soapy water using a bottle and teat brush to remove all milk and powder.

- Place in a large saucepan, covered with water and remove all air bubbles in bottles.

- Bring to the boil for five minutes then allow to cool in the water to avoid burns or use clean tongs to remove.

- Any equipment not required immediately can be stored in a container in the fridge.
- All equipment should be boiled/sterilised within 24 hours of being used.

This was the method we used and my husband started an evening routine of boiling up all of the equipment, I think at the time he enjoyed having a 'job' to do and it helped to share the workload.

Electric steam sterilisers

- Wash bottles, teats, caps and other feeding equipment in warm soapy water using a bottle and teat brush to remove all milk and powder.
- Place inside unit and add correct amount of water, follow instructions for use.
- Switch on.
- Unit will turn off automatically.
- Important to remove any excess water left over after each use.
- Any equipment not required immediately can be stored in the steriliser or in a container in the fridge.
- All feeding equipment should be sterilised within 24 hours of being used.

Microwave steam sterilisers

- Wash bottles, teats, caps and other feeding equipment in warm soapy water using a bottle and teat brush to remove all milk and powder.
- Place inside unit and add correct amount of water, follow instructions.
- Microwave for recommended time period.
- Any equipment not required immediately can be stored in the steriliser or in a container in the fridge.

- All feeding equipment should be sterilised within 24 hours of being used.

Feeding equipment should be sterilised until your baby is at least six months of age, after this age your baby will be eating solids as well as putting unsterile toys and other objects into their mouths so simply washing with hot soapy water and rinsing will be sufficient. Many parents continue to sterilise until 12 months out of personal choice.

How much formula does my baby need?

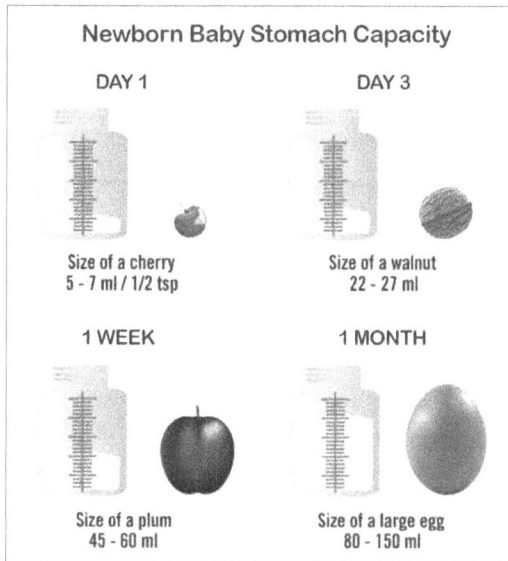

Newborn Baby Stomach Capacity

DAY 1 — Size of a cherry 5 - 7 ml / 1/2 tsp

DAY 3 — Size of a walnut 22 - 27 ml

1 WEEK — Size of a plum 45 - 60 ml

1 MONTH — Size of a large egg 80 - 150 ml

The first few feeds after birth should be small, as your baby's stomach is about the size of a cherry, only offer 10–20 ml to start with and then increase to 50 ml gradually as tolerated over the first few days. If your baby is tolerating this well and crying and looking for more go ahead and try a little more each feed. If your baby drinks too much he will probably vomit as his stomach has been overstretched, give a little less next feed.

Over the next month many babies will drink around 80–120 ml of formula each feed, remember this is dependent on how often your baby feeds and how big they are.

Chapter 5: Bottle feeding

From around one to two months of age many babies will drink around 150 ml each feed, two to four months up to 200 ml and from four months and beyond up to 250 ml.

Formula tin labels have suggestions of bottle feed amounts for different aged babies, remember to use this as a guide only, many babies regardless of age never drink more than 180 ml but most cans suggest giving up to 250 ml each feed. As long as your baby is growing and developing well over time, there is no need to force milk into them. Your child and family health nurse, doctor or paediatrician will let you know if there is any concern with your babies growth, be guided by them.

As your baby grows and starts solid foods she will need less formula over time. From around eight months of age you can begin to offer meals before bottles.

How to bottle feed my baby

For a healthy full-term baby, rather than timing bottle feeds it is best to be led by your baby, this is called demand feeding. Look for hunger cues from your baby, these may include opening her mouth and trying to look for a nipple, wanting to suck on anything such as her hands, your arm, fussing and crying. By responding to these cues early your baby will learn to trust you and be more settled.

If your baby was premature or has been slow to gain weight your health professional may instruct you to wake your baby regularly and give you an amount of formula to try to feed your baby each time. It is important to follow this feeding plan. Once she is gaining weight, your health professional will let you know when you can move to demand feeding.

Check the formula temperature on your inner wrist, it should feel lukewarm not hot. If hot, immerse sealed bottle in cold water.

Cradle your baby in your arms, keep her head above her body and offer the bottle by touching the teat on her lips until she opens her mouth wide,

then put the teat filled with milk, no air, in gently – she will probably start to suck immediately as this is a reflex action. Never force the bottle into her mouth, she may not be hungry and she may come to dislike bottle feeding. While she is sucking check that her lips are flanged outwards, you can gently fix this with your fingers. Milk should not be escaping around the edges, this could require the use of a different style of teat.

Give her a break when her sucking slows or she becomes overwhelmed, and gently burp her either by patting her back while over your shoulder or sitting up on your lap with her chin supported – if after a few minutes she has not burped you can stop. Offer her the bottle again, she may or may not want more, look for her pushing the teat out with her tongue, pursing her lips shut, gagging, crying, don't force her to finish it. If she wants a small feed sometimes and larger feeds other times that is normal but if she is not taking enough to grow adequately you will need to try to get bigger feeds in, again be guided by your health professional. Aim to complete a feed within one hour at most, some babies need a nappy change halfway to wake them up, then discard any leftover milk.

Most babies will vomit a little milk up after a feed, the muscle at the top of her stomach is still developing, you can put a burp cloth/cloth nappy over your shoulder ready for this, this will improve with age.

Never prop your baby up with a bottle, you should always hold the bottle for your baby and be able to attend to her if she has trouble coping with the flow or needs to burp.

One of the benefits of breastfeeding is better eye development, this can be mimicked when bottle feeding by alternating arms when feeding allowing equal development of her eyes.

How much weight should my baby gain?

This very much depends on your baby, their birth weight, your feeding method, genetics and any medical conditions that they may have.

In the early days, it is normal for your baby to lose up to 10% of their birth weight in the first week but we aim for them to have regained this by two weeks of age.

Early weight checks should be at least 48 hours apart to avoid unnecessarily alarming the parents, as your baby could appear to have lost weight due to time of weight check before or after a feed, passing urine or having a large bowel movement prior to weighing.

Sometimes there can be discrepancy between scales from the hospital, home visiting scales, GP's office, nurses centre. If this may have occurred, try to use the same scales for most future weight checks. No weight gain or loss of weight over a few days must be taken seriously and a check of bottle feeding technique, formula type, amount, frequency of feeds and if this is all normal then a medical examination is required to exclude medical illness.

The best way to monitor growth over time is by using a growth chart, in Australia the World Health Organization (WHO) growth charts are usually used and we expect babies to grow in a similar curve to that on the graph. If a baby seems to be crossing percentiles particularly downward an assessment of feeding and a medical examination is required.

Average weight gain	
Birth to 3 months	150–200 gms a week
3 to 6 months	100–150 gms a week
6-12 months	70–90 gms a week

Don't be alarmed if your baby is not gaining exactly this amount, be guided by your health care professional and if you are worried get a second opinion.

When to stop bottle feeding

After 12 months formula is not required, full cream cow's milk can be used, it is best to gradually change to this. Some babies don't like the taste of cow's milk so you can mix some formula with the cow's milk and gradually reduce the amount of formula until your baby drinks only full cream cow's milk.

Most bottle fed babies love their bottle, I can distinctly remember my first baby calling hers "bobble" when she wanted it, it was so cute. Bottles are a difficult thing to remove from many babies due to this love. After 12 months of age it is good to move to a sippy cup rather than a bottle as bottles encourage babies to skull large amounts of milk and your baby no longer requires this, she should be getting most of her nutrition from eating a broad range of family foods including dairy.

Many babies continue on with the bedtime bottle until well after 12 months as it has become part of the bedtime routine, unfortunately many of these babies get dental cavities from the sugar in the milk sitting against their teeth all night. Please clean your baby's teeth gently with a soft toothbrush and water after the night time bottle, this can be done quietly in dim light so she remains drowsy.

Websites

- www.raisingchildren.net.au
- www.betterhealth.vic.gov.au

Chapter 6

Moving on to solid foods

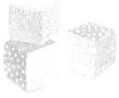

Chapter 6

Moving on to solid foods

> *"The aim of introducing solid food is to have your baby eating what you eat by 12 months of age"*
> **Belinda Joyce**

Moving on to solid food

The introduction of solid foods has been a changing landscape over the past ten years with inconsistent advice from health professional's due to new research and guidelines both nationally and internationally. Much of the research has been centred around reducing the rates of food allergies which have sky rocketed in the past 10–20 years. The latest Australian National Health and Medical Research Council (NHMRC) guidelines have a more relaxed approach around introducing solids compared to previous guidelines which had many rules and made introducing variety more difficult.

When to start solids

We know all babies require solid foods somewhere around six months of age, but not before four months.

Be watching for signs of readiness such as:

- Being able to sit with support.
- Having good head control.

- Watching you eat with an increased level of interest.

- Making you feel guilty for eating in front of them.

- Drooling when watching you.

- Reaching out to take your food.

- Copying a chewing motion.

- Opening mouth when food is offered.

Once you are seeing some of these signs this is the time to start, as it is a window where your baby is very interested and likely to enjoy eating and be willing to try a variety of foods. Starting solid foods with your baby should be a fun, new activity, if your baby is not enjoying it and it is becoming stressful wait a week and try again. Eating is a social time in our society and babies will usually enjoy joining in, especially if others are eating at the same time. If you have not seen any signs of readiness at six months, start solids, as your baby will need more nutrition than just breastmilk or formula alone.

Breastmilk or infant formula remains your baby's most important source of nutrition until closer to twelve months of age.

Which foods to introduce first

You can start with any foods you would like, the only exception to this is honey, until your baby is over twelve months of age, due to the risk of botulism, a rare but potentially fatal condition that causes progressive weakness.

The texture of foods given to baby's needs to be based on their developmental stage, for example young babies from four months of age manage pureed foods better than foods which require more chewing. The first few meals your baby has may include some gagging as he gets used to managing the food in his mouth and moves it to the back of his tongue to swallow. The texture of the puree should be gradually increased to a

lumpy consistency by seven months so that your baby learns to chew, these same muscles are used for speech. If you continue to give smooth puree until later, many baby's will refuse anything with lumps, gag and have difficulty moving on to the next stage. Avoid hard foods such as nuts and raw carrot, as these are a choking hazard.

Iron-rich and iron-fortified foods are a good place to start, as iron is important for brain development. In the past, rice cereal was often suggested as the first food and there is nothing wrong with it, however once your baby has eaten foods with more flavour they may never want plain rice cereal again – try it yourself, it is very bland but can be mixed in with other foods as a thickener, as it is rich in iron. Other forms of iron rich foods are meat, including beef, lamb, pork, chicken and fish as well as tofu and legumes. There is no reason to wait until your baby is older to start meat.

Dieticians believe there is value in giving your baby single flavours to begin with as an educational experience such as sweet potato, pumpkin, carrot, peas, apples and pears, but within a few weeks of eating solids start giving family meals whenever possible so your baby gets exposed to variety, with different flavours and textures. Only one small meal a day is needed to begin with.

Try to limit salt and sugar if possible by removing baby's food before this is added. Herbs and spices are a better way to give flavour and are good to be introduced. If your family eats spicy foods start with mild flavours and gradually increase the intensity, by twelve months your baby will probably tolerate moderate heat, the addition of natural or Greek yoghurt can help to reduce the intensity.

To puree family meals you can use a food processor or stick blender. For example, if you are preparing spaghetti Bolognese for dinner you can just put some in a food processor and whiz it up into a puree for your baby to try, pasta, meat sauce and all. Some foods need a few tablespoons of boiled water to help them blend smoothly.

Chapter 6: Moving on to solid foods

Even if you use jars of sauces or recipe base packets to help with meal preparation these are generally still safe for your baby – do read the ingredient label first but most are a mix of herbs, spices, tomato puree, cream and water.

Any egg, meat or fish should be well cooked in the first year to avoid illness.

Try to cook your baby's foods yourself from fresh, frozen or canned ingredients, by moving to family meals this is easier, as you only need to prepare one meal. When you make a large meal that purees easily, store some extra portions in the freezer for those times when you may have something that doesn't blend up such as a salad.

It is important for your baby to have foods from all food groups such as fruit, vegetables, protein such as meats and eggs, carbohydrates such as pasta, rice, breads and full fat dairy such as yoghurt and cheese. Many families I see, give their baby a mixture of vegetables only, every night and this is not giving them all the variety they need.

In the early days the amount of food most baby's consume is very small, you may only start with a teaspoon and gradually increase this based on your baby's cues. Early feeding is a learning experience and quantity is not important, if your baby only has one spoonful and then closes their mouth and won't let any more in, that is fine. Babies often need to be offered a new food many times before they will learn to like it. If your baby wants more, give them more, they are very good at knowing when they have had enough, be guided by behaviour.

Full fat cow's milk can be used on your baby's cereal and in small quantities in other foods such as mashed potato, however breastmilk or infant formula remain your baby's main drink until 12 months of age.

Once solids have begun it is nice to offer your baby some cooled boiled water from a sippy cup with meals, it is refreshing to have a drink when eating. Please avoid fruit juices, soft drinks, tea, coffee, rice and soy drinks.

Baby-led weaning

Baby-led weaning (BLW) is letting your baby feed himself, the food is not pureed and it is usually done around the dinner table from the parents plate. Some parents believe this is a more natural process for introducing solid foods. There is no need for special preparation of baby food as you are only offering what the rest of the family is eating.

As your baby will not have developed a pincer grip at this young age, you can try to offer foods that he will be able to clasp, such as broccoli florets, where he can use the stem like a handle, toast crusts, pieces of tender meat.

This method allows baby to explore different foods textures, flavours and decide what to eat and how much. Always stay close by in case of choking.

Many parents are passionate about this method of introducing solids as their babies generally eat anything offered and they believe it encourages better food habits later in life, however there is currently no clear evidence of this.

BLW starts off as a messy process and to begin with, much food is only played with and therefore limited nutrients ingested by baby. From six months on baby's need the addition of iron rich foods such as meat, as breastmilk alone will not meet this need, some health professionals worry that BLW will not meet these needs.

Dieticians generally state that a wide variety of textures are important when introducing solid foods so including some sloppy or pureed foods can be educational and important for acceptance later in life.

Whichever method you choose to use, see your child health nurse or doctor if you have any concerns.

What about commercial foods?

Commercially available baby foods can be very convenient, however you don't always know what is in it and it does not taste like real family foods, particularly the savoury foods such as meat and vegetables – have a taste for yourself you will see what I mean. It is often made into a very smooth puree, smoother than anything you could prepare at home. Move on to the varieties aimed at six months plus to ensure some texture and continue to move on to eight months plus soon after. Some ready-made baby foods are on the shelf in the supermarket while others are in the freezer section.

Buying prepared baby food is an expensive way of feeding your baby and it does not teach your baby to eat the kinds of foods your family eat. If you do like to buy baby food please feed your baby with a spoon rather than squirting pureed food from a pouch into your baby's mouth, we want your baby to be able to see the colour and to open his mouth ready to enjoy it.

If holidaying in another country where food standards are lower than those in Australia, taking some commercial baby food is very helpful in keeping your baby well.

Ready-made food can be handy to have in the nappy bag when you are out and about, as much of it does not need to be refrigerated, don't forget to put in a spoon as well.

More brands are coming onto the Australian market offering boutique style baby meals, coming out of smaller factories, using more common processes to home cooking and generally better and more interesting ingredients.

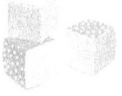

What about food allergies?

The experts currently agree, that withholding possible allergenic foods until a later age does not reduce food allergy, therefore it is important to expose your baby to as many different foods as possible. This includes dairy: milk, yoghurt, cheese; egg, nuts – but not whole nuts as these are a choking hazard, try spreads such as peanut butter, hazelnut spread, almond and cashew spreads or even almond meal which can be added to their food. Try these potential allergenic foods soon after starting solids and continue to offer them throughout their first year of life.

This is important even if there is a family history of food allergy. Although babies with a family history of food allergy are more at risk, any baby can develop an allergy. Some parents I see have been very worried due to another child in the family having severe food allergies and so they have given their baby an allergenic food close to the hospital just in case medical treatment was needed.

By continuing to breastfeed during the introduction of foods, your baby will have some protection to developing allergies.

The skin on your baby's face is sensitive and may become irritated by some foods such as tomatoes, citrus, berries, other fruit and vegemite – this is not a food allergy. Some health professionals used to suggest smearing food on baby's face to check for allergy, however this does not help to identify food allergy.

If your baby has an allergic reaction to any foods, it is important to stop that food and see your doctor and don't give this food to your baby again without medical advice. If your baby has a reaction that makes breathing difficult call an ambulance immediately on 000 in Australia.

Much more research is needed on food allergy prevention.

Chapter 6: Moving on to solid foods

Seven to eight months plus

From around eight months you can start to offer meals before breast or bottle feeds, over the course of a day his milk needs will reduce. If he is not already eating three meals a day, now is the time to increase to this, between now and 12 months of age you can add in healthy snacks as well.

Give your baby his own spoon to learn to use while you continue to feed him from another spoon, this will encourage self-feeding.

Although your baby will probably continue to eat lumpy or even fork mashed food from a spoon, now is the time to try some finger foods – toast crusts are a great way to try this. Inevitably he will put finger foods too far into his mouth and gag a number of times before he learns to manage this new skill, but don't worry he will usually pull it back out himself. I know I really worried about my baby choking, but chances are by the time you try to help them clear their throat they will be fine and looking at you, wondering why you look so worried. Do stay close by when your baby is eating so that you can help if needed.

You can cut food into a good shape so your baby can hold one end and chew on the other. Anything can be a finger food including pasta spirals and tubes, cooked vegetable pieces such as carrot sticks, pieces of cooked meat, teething rusks.

As your baby learns to eat finger foods he is going to make a mess, try to relax and let him enjoy touching and playing with his food, this is all part of learning to eat and developing healthy habits with food.

Baby's do not need processed foods such as chips, cakes, fried foods, biscuits, it is best to avoid these until after 12 months if possible.

What if I want my baby to be vegetarian or vegan

A vegetarian diet alone does not provide enough iron or zinc for an infant, so they need iron fortified cereals, milks and other foods. Vegan diets also lack vitamin B12 which is only found in animal foods. Iron and zinc are required for optimal brain development.

For those on a vegan diet breastfeeding for as long as possible, two years or more if desired is recommended. If formula fed, a soy based formula for the first two years of life is recommended.

It is best to see a dietician to ensure your baby is getting enough iron and other nutrients from their food. Many vegan infants will require iron and B12 supplements and possibly more.

Some first recipes to try

Vegetable purees:

Pumpkin puree: half a small pumpkin, butternut, jap or other.

Sweet potato puree: 1 medium

- Peel and cut vegetables into 2–3 cm cubes.
- Boil, steam or microwave with a small amount of water until soft.
- Blend with a stick blender, food processor or push through a sieve. If vegetable puree needs more thinning use boiled water, breast milk or formula.

Meat, such as mince beef, casserole beef, chicken thigh or breast fillets can be added and many other vegetables using the same principles, ensure meat is cooked through. Boiling/simmering works best when adding meat, casserole meats need longer cooking times to become tender.

Fruit purees:

Apple puree: 2 apples, peeled, cored and sliced, granny smith, golden delicious or other variety

Pear puree: 2 pears, peeled, cored and sliced.

Place in a saucepan with 3 tablespoons of water and bring to the boil over medium heat, gently simmer for 10 minutes, fruit should be very soft.

Remove from heat, allow to cool for 10 minutes then blend with a stick blender, food processor or push through a sieve. If fruit puree needs more thinning use boiled water, breast milk or formula. Great added to rice or any baby cereal.

Try adding berries, peaches or apricots. Fruit can be fresh, frozen or canned.

Once your baby has been on solid foods for a few weeks try to use family foods wherever possible rather than making separate 'baby' foods.

Websites

NHMRC EAT FOR HEALTH Infant Feeding Guidelines SUMMARY:

https://www.eatforhealth.gov.au/sites/default/files/files/the_guidelines/
n56b_infant_feeding_summary_130808.pdf

How to Make Every Bite Count, a good publication on introducing solids
with recipes and shows how to adapt family meals:

http://www.beefandlamb.com.au/Learn/Online_magazines/How_to_
make_every_bite_count

raisingchildren.net.au: has recipes and pictures to give ideas and
inspiration.

kidspot.com.au: recipe ideas

Chapter 7

Crying, sleep and settling

Chapter 7

Crying, sleep and settling

> *"Crying is your baby's language and a communication that he needs something or someone to help him feel safe and secure."*
> **Pinky McKay**

Crying

All babies cry, it is your baby's most effective form of communication and is for many parents the most difficult part of early parenting. When I had my first baby the best piece of parenting advice I got from a very dear friend was that babies cry, that's just what they do and just because my baby was crying a lot it wasn't because I was doing anything wrong. To be honest at the time I felt like a failure and this new 'parenting thing' was not feeling like the baby commercials on TV had led me to believe at all!

In the early weeks and months you are still getting to know your baby so it is important to go to them when they are distressed and crying to check what they need. You can't spoil your baby by attending to them promptly, in fact your baby is not necessarily crying to make you come, he is crying because he has a problem. If you can solve the problem for him or just be there to offer support, he will learn to cope in difficult times.

It has been well documented that newborn babies cry a little more each day and will most likely peak at around six to eight weeks of age, with many hours of inconsolable crying each day, often in the evening when parents are also tired. These bouts of crying often last 20–40 mins but can

last hours at a time. Many well-meaning friends and family will tell you that you will get to know your baby's cries, but in the early weeks much of the crying is inconsolable and the baby will often sound distressed with every cry, and a strategy to soothe your baby that works one day may not work the next. The crying itself often seems to have no obvious cause and is resistant to soothing efforts which make it very frustrating. Most babies appear to be in pain but after medical assessment almost all will have no medical cause. If you are at all concerned see you doctor for a thorough check of your baby to rule out any medical cause.

Experts are unable to determine a cause for this crying, however it appears to be a normal part of behavioural development and it is reassuring to know that your baby is normal if he is following this pattern. If only more parents were told about this, as just knowing that it is normal can make it easier to cope with.

There is always a lot of talk about wind with babies but much of the wind is probably caused from all the bouts of crying where the baby swallows large amounts of air.

Colic is a term that often comes up around wind and crying, this usually causes a more severe form of inconsolable crying which goes on for longer, where the baby draws his legs up and appears to have severe abdominal pain, see the 'Caring for your baby' chapter for more information on colic.

Know that this time will pass and that you just have to get through it. Some babies have a more demanding temperament than others but most babies will be crying much less by three months of age. By this age you are more likely to know why your baby is crying, this is partly because your own confidence has grown as you have gotten to know your baby better and partly because the cries will be less often and different, not just a distressed cry every time. Also it seems that babies digestive systems have often settled and matured by this age. Most parents find they really start to enjoy parenting much more when they can figure out why their baby is crying, and by addressing the reason, stop them crying.

Possible reasons for crying:

- **Hunger**

  Offer a feed, see breast or bottle feeding chapters.

- **Wants to suck**

  If fed recently offer a dummy or babies own fingers.

- **Needs comfort and closeness from parent**

  Pick up baby and cuddle, try rhythmic patting, rocking, shushing noises.

- **Uncomfortable**

  Too hot or cold, change position, clothing.

- **Tired or overtired**

  Read on for sleep and settling information.

- **Dirty nappy or nappy rash**

  Check nappy, change and apply a nappy barrier cream.

- **Wind or digestive pain or discomfort in the tummy**

  Try gentle tummy massage, cycle legs, cuddle as your warm body acts as a heat pack to baby's tummy.

- **Needs to burp**

  Lift into upright position over shoulder or sitting up on your lap, gently pat and rub back.

- **Overstimulated by visitors, TV, loud noises**

  Reduce stimulation, dim lighting, quiet noises, TV off.

- **Teething**

  Gently rub gums, check for inflamed area, see 'Caring for your baby' chapter.

- **Illness, fever or feeling miserable**

  See 'Caring for your baby' chapter.

- **Parent is distressed or angry/upset**

  Ask for help or if home alone place your baby into the cot and take a short break, make a cup of tea, step outside for some fresh air, phone a friend, take three deep breaths, this will make your body calm a little. When you go back to your baby he will probably still be crying but you will be more able to cope with the crying.

IF DISTRESSED:

Never shake your baby this can cause irreversible brain damage as the brain bounces around in the skull. If you are feeling frustrated, angry or overwhelmed please ask for help from family, friends or health professionals. New parents sometimes find it difficult to manage their emotions especially when feeling overwhelmed and sleep deprived.

Many parents I speak to are shocked when I mention that they may have these strong emotions and that I myself have felt completely overwhelmed in the early weeks with three out of my four babies! My husband often comments on the mental and emotional strain he faced particularly with our second child who would rarely settle for him. He recalls with great disappointment, pacing the room with our crying son as his frustration would build. He would place the baby in the cot and storm away furious not just at our son but also at himself. Talking with your partner about these feelings can help you feel better, you are not alone.

Please consider the 'Time out' strategy for your own wellbeing as much as for the child.

> *"People who say they sleep like a baby usually don't have one."*
> **Leo J Burke, psychologist**

Sleep and Settling

We all need to sleep, it's a basic human need, but babies need to sleep much more than adults and it is during sleep that they grow and develop. It is understandable that we want our babies to sleep well, after all sleep deprivation is used as a form of torture. However, it is important to understand how babies sleep and what to do to improve sleep problems.

Babies who don't get enough sleep are often over-tired and grizzly, they are more difficult to settle and may not reach developmental milestones as soon because they find it harder to learn.

We must have realistic expectations, night feeds are a reality up until around six months of age for many babies. Newborns have small stomachs and often need to feed two to four hourly and sometimes more, especially during a growth spurt. Babies require many sleeps and naps each day.

Safe Sleep

Experts recommend your baby to sleep in a cot in the parents' bedroom. It is better to go into a full-sized cot from birth as these have safety standards and are therefore safer for your baby.

The benefits of sleeping your baby in your room include, having them close for feeds and settling as well as being able to check on them more easily and more often.

Safe sleeping guidelines:

Always sleep your baby on the back.

Sleep in a safe cot in parents' room for the first 6–12 months.

Breastfeed your baby if able.

Keep head and face uncovered. Make up cot short-sheeted with baby's feet at bottom and sheets and blankets tucked in firmly with no loose sheets, so they can't wriggle down under the sheets. Use of a swaddle or sleeping bag can help with this.

Dress your baby in warm clothing but not hot so they won't overheat.

Never sleep baby on couches, makeshift bedding or in parents arms where there is a risk of falling asleep themselves.

Keep baby's environment smoke free before and after birth.

Source: Red Nose

Ensure all your baby's carers know how to sleep your baby safely.

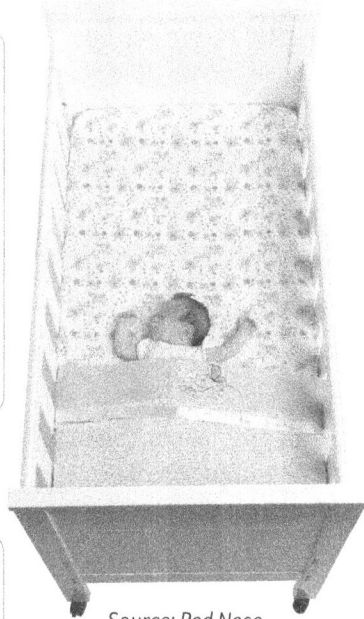

Safe sleep environment during the day and night: safe cot, firm, clean, right-sized mattress. Safe bedding, no quilts, woollen underlays, cot bumpers, wedges, soft toys or pillows.

Using a safe sleeping bag keeps baby on back longer and therefore assists with risk reduction.

SIDS & SUDI

The following risk factors are associated with most sudden unexpected deaths in infancy (SUDI) including sudden infant death syndrome (SIDS) and fatal sleep accidents in both Australia and abroad:

- Sleeping on tummy or side.

- Face and head covered with bedding leading to overheating or asphyxia.

- Smoking during pregnancy or after birth.

- Soft sleep surfaces, woollen underlays, water beds, pillows, soft mattresses.

By implementing the safe sleeping guidelines your baby will be much safer.

Temperature: put two fingers down onto baby's chest to check, if hot or sweaty they are too hot, reduce clothing or blankets. Checking hand or foot temperature does not give a true indication as often these are cold, especially when asleep.

Room temperature: the main danger is becoming too hot as this has been associated with SUDI. In hot weather if you don't have air conditioning, you can try using of a pedestal fan and using light clothing on your baby.

Keep cords from blinds, mobiles and electrical appliances away from the cot, as your baby gets older they will try to reach and pull things into their cot.

Clothing for sleep: clothing to sleep your baby in should be simple, comfortable and breathable fabrics with no hood or decorative lace which could become tangled or dangerous for your baby. A singlet or similar and one more layer of clothing is generally enough, I found an all in one suit the most comfortable and practical for changing nappies. In very hot weather only one layer such as a singlet and nappy only is

best. No hats or hoods should be worn during sleep, these can overheat your baby.

Safe wrapping/swaddling: Swaddling helps your baby to feel confined and secure as they were in the womb, it also reduces the chance of rolling. There are many different methods of wrapping but as long as it is firm over the upper body to contain the hands and loose around the hips so that your baby's legs can fall open in a frog-like position this will enable normal hip development. Always use 100% cotton, cotton jersey or muslin as it breathes well and in hot weather reduce clothing layers.

As your baby loses the startle reflex, start to reduce wrapping, leave arms out and wrap from chest down. Once your baby can roll, often around four months of age, stop wrapping as she can become entangled in the wraps. Sometimes this needs to be a gentle transition as your baby may be used to being swaddled and may not settle without this security.

Red Nose do not recommend the use of swaddle bags that restrict movement and pin a baby in a position with arms in. A safe sleeping bag with arms out is a safer option.

Swaddle bags are popular as no wrapping skills are required, make sure these are the correct size for your baby and not too large as their head could slip down into the bag. Once your baby is rolling they need to have their hands and arms out.

Reflux

Even if your baby suffers from reflux and vomiting, which is very common in babies less than three months of age, it is still safest to sleep them flat on their back rather than tilting or elevating the mattress, as their protective mechanisms work best in this position. Any vomit is likely to go back down into the stomach and not into their airways. Elevating the cot actually increases the risk of your baby slipping down into the blankets. The benefit of keeping milk down is not enough to risk SUDI. In particular circumstances a paediatrician may suggest elevating the cot

or other sleep positions other than back sleeping however this should take into account safe sleeping guidelines and the baby's medical needs, in my experience this does not happen often.

(✗) On Front   (✓) On Back

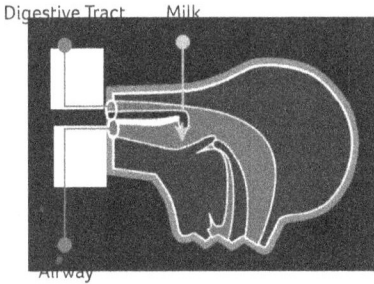
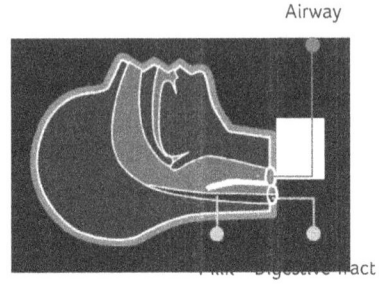

Source: Red Nose

Sleep science

Babies sleep cycles are very different to ours, they last between 20–50 minutes, starting with alert, down into a deep sleep then lightens into REM phase. At the end of each cycle babies usually wake very briefly, this is when many babies require assistance to go back down into a deep sleep

Light sleep: REM phase, your baby may look like he's dreaming, wriggle, twitch, can see eyes moving under lids, irregular breathing.

Deep sleep: Non-REM, deeper regular breathing, very still, occasional sucking, hard to wake, drowsy.

Between REM and non-REM babies rouse a little and can appear to be awake, even with their eyes open.

Babies, due to having shorter sleep cycles, spend much of their sleep time in light sleep and wake more often. With age, the periods of light sleep decrease and over time more deep sleep occurs.

The aim is to help your baby to sleep through one sleep cycle and into the next, providing at least one hours' sleep during day naps and longer overnight, this will provide over 24 hours, adequate rest so they can rest, grow and develop to their full potential.

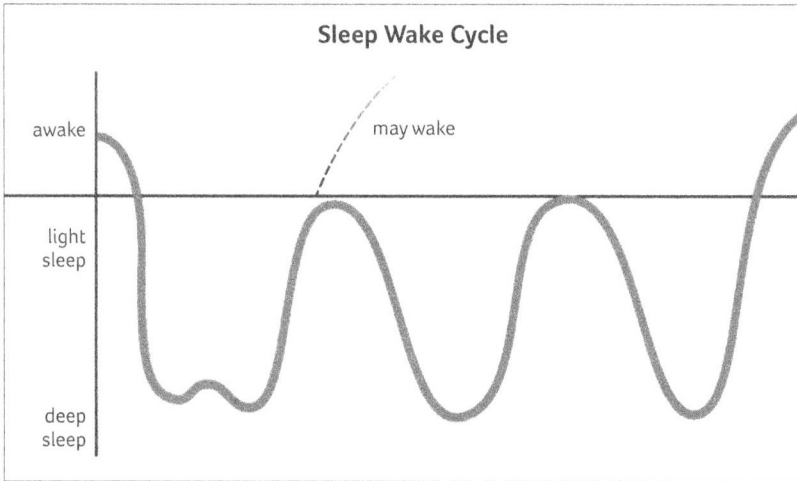

Sleep Wake Cycle

awake

may wake

light sleep

deep sleep

Newborns often sleep around 16 hours every 24 hours. They usually wake 2-3 times overnight and require feeding.

Average sleep requirements			
Age	Day sleep	Night sleep	Average total sleep
Newborn	8–9 hrs (3–5 naps)	8–9 hrs	16–18 hrs
1–2 months	6–7 hrs (3–4 naps)	8–9 hrs	14–16 hrs
3–5 months	4–5 hrs (3 naps)	10–11 hrs	14–16 hrs
6–8 months	3–5 hrs (3 naps)	10–11 hrs	14–15 hrs
9–11 months	2.5–4 hrs (2–3 naps)	11–12 hrs	13–15 hrs
12 months	2–3 hrs (1–2 naps)	11–12 hrs	13–14 hrs

Remember these are just averages, as with adults some babies require more and some require less. The key is that if your baby is showing tired signs then they need more sleep.

Newborn tired signs

- Jerky movements
- Crying, grizzling
- Fist clenching
- Turning face away, dazed
- Yawning
- Coughing/choking/hiccups
- Back arching

- Squirming/kicking aggressively
- Vomiting/possiting
- Red around eyes or eyebrows
- Hands to mouth
- Dark circles under eyes
- Facial grimacing
- Clinginess

Helping your newborn to sleep

If your baby is premature or slow to gain weight your paediatrician or nurse may suggest not allowing them to sleep too long in order to get adequate feeds in for growth, you can still use these basic concepts but please be guided by your health professionals.

Babies that learn to sleep independently within the first 12 weeks have less sleep problems in their first year. A baby who sleeps independently can sleep for longer periods, cycling in and out of light and deep sleep, resettling themselves. Most newborn babies up to at least four months will still require feeding overnight but can still be independent sleepers, lengthening out their sleeps particularly overnight and going back to sleep soon after feeds. Any changes you make to your baby's sleep before 12 weeks are easier on your baby and yourself.

Some families worry that aiming for independent sleep is going to hurt their baby emotionally, however there is currently no evidence to suggest this and as long as there is plenty of cuddling, touching and love during the day and you are responsive and sensitive with the approach, your baby will still know they are loved. However we all have different feelings and this is a decision for you to make. Sleep is important for baby and parents

and getting enough sleep reduces the incidence of postnatal depression and anxiety.

Once your newborn baby has been awake for 1–1.5 hours, they will probably be showing some tired signs. Tired signs are often easier to see if baby is not in your arms, as while he is in your arms he is distracted by you, put him on a rug on the floor and sit next to him. Once you have seen a few tired signs it is time to make him comfortable and ready for sleep. If the only tired sign you have seen is crying and you're not sure if your baby is tired or hungry, go ahead and give them another feed, particularly if it's over two hours since his last feed. When your baby gets older the tired signs will be easier to recognise.

Check your baby's needs have been met, nappy dry, fed well, had some play/awake time. Swaddle for young baby, this helps to avoid the startle reflex which is a strong jerky movement that will often wake your baby and make him hit himself in the face. After four months your baby may be rolling and it is no longer safe to swaddle due to the risk of entanglement and suffocation, a sleeping bag works well to reduce rolling and to keep baby warm and comfortable.

By creating a simple routine before putting your baby into the cot she will learn that sleep time is coming, it is good if this is something all carers of your baby can also do. Some quiet time before sleep will also assist your baby to get ready for sleep – turn off screens, if music is playing make sure it's relaxing, speak in a calm quiet voice, sing a lullaby, reduce eye contact as this may 'rev him up' for play. If your baby is drowsy when put into the cot in the early weeks of learning to sleep and self soothe in their cot they are likely to settle more easily.

A darkened room has less distractions meaning better sleep for most babies.

Put him into his cot awake but ready for sleep, always on his back and with feet at the end of the cot. Say goodnight, give him a kiss. It is better to start in the cot as when he gets into light sleep and realises he is in the

cot and this is not where he was when he fell asleep this can be upsetting and confusing causing further crying and attention.

Give your baby the opportunity to go to sleep himself, he may need some time to stretch and wriggle a little, sometimes vocalising, grizzling before he is able to fall asleep. I know when I go to bed I often need to read a few pages of a book before I'm ready to fall asleep!

Sometimes it may feel as if your newborn is crying for you to come, however they don't understand that you exist when they can't see you, therefore they are crying because they require attention or can't fall asleep themselves and need some help.

What if your newborn baby is tired, unsettled and crying?

First run through a quick mental checklist – has he had a good feed recently, is his nappy clean, has he had some awake time? Meet these needs first. If your baby is grizzling that is fine and normal but if he is crying in distress then it is best to stay with them and try some soothing strategies, such as patting or double-patting at a similar rate as your heartbeat. Just because your baby is crying does not mean you must pick them up immediately. We don't want your baby to be left alone and feeling abandoned when distressed, however staying and helping them to go to sleep can work well.

You can pat him tummy, side, the mattress, if not improving you can roll him onto his side and pat his upper back or bottom area, many babies really enjoy this. Double-patting on the bottom or thighs and shoulder or upper back. Rhythmic patting often works well. Make sure you leave your baby on his back for sleep.

You can also try gentle and slow body rocking holding your baby's shoulder and hip. Once he is calming, try quietly leaving him to drop off to sleep himself. This is teaching your baby to self-soothe. By using 'in cot' settling methods we avoid picking up and cuddling so that she will learn to drop off to sleep in her cot, this is the beginning of learning to self-soothe.

If you are using a dummy this can be used throughout the settling process as well, many babies have a very strong urge to suck, especially when going to sleep, it has a soothing effect.

If your baby wakes under one hour then it is a good idea to try to resettle them in the cot to get a longer sleep, using the same settling strategies discussed earlier.

Some parents prefer to walk, feed, cuddle and rock their baby to sleep and this is nice to do sometimes, but if you do this every time this is how your baby will learn to go to sleep and keep requiring this each time they are in light sleep to get back to sleep.

At some stage during this process you may begin to feel angry and frustrated, this is normal. Leave your baby in the cot and take a few minutes to yourself, walk outside and get some fresh air or make a cup of tea. Then go back and try again, if this is happening regularly please ask for help from your maternal and child health nurse, GP or paediatrician.

See the crying chapter for some more strategies to use when your baby is crying and you are not able to get him to sleep.

If at any time deep down you feel this settling technique is not right for you and your baby you should stop immediately, this may be a good time to have a discussion with your child health nurse about sleep and settling and consider some support with this. See sleep resource section at the end of this chapter for Early Parenting Centre contact details in each state and you may have local services such as day stay programs.

Dream or rollover feeds can help, this is a feed late in the evening often before you go to bed yourself. You wake your baby quietly and feed them in the darkened room then put them back into the cot drowsy, avoid a nappy change if able. This can help to extend the uninterrupted period of sleep overnight. Many parents swear by this method however some babies, mine included have particular times they will wake and giving them this later top-up may make no difference.

Feed Play Sleep routine

Using the feed, play, sleep routine may help, it creates a predictable pattern for both parent and baby and calmer brain patterns for babies. It needs to be used in a flexible and gentle way rather than being rigid, particularly with a newborn. Try to begin this pattern before 12 weeks if possible.

Feed, play, sleep is an easily reproduced routine for parents and carers which does not rely solely on mothers.

Daytime feed/play/sleep cycle

Feed

Feed baby when they wake, this becomes the beginning of the cycle. Because your baby has just woken they often feed better as they have more energy, often they have woken because they are hungry.

Play

Playtime for a very small baby does not need to be particularly structured it may just be talking to your baby while they are on the change table, smiling, telling them about the world, or it may be down on the floor on a mat under a play gym looking at toys hanging. It is also a great opportunity for some tummy time while they are awake and supervised, this will help to strengthen back, neck and arm muscles.

While your baby is playing look for tired signs as discussed earlier in the chapter, once you see a few it is time for sleep. It is easier to see the tired signs if your baby is not in your arms. Try to avoid over stimulating your baby close to sleep time, turn the television off, talk quietly and calmly, no bright lights. See the 'Play and Development' chapter for more play ideas.

Sleep

Make sure you have met your baby's needs, nappy is dry and then put them in their cot for sleep, wrap if this is your preference.

The aim is for a sleep of at least one to two hours but no more than four hours during the day as we want to encourage the longer sleeps during the night. Having said this, a baby that sleeps well during the day will sleep better at night as sleep promotes sleep.

Over time as baby grows and matures the play periods will extend before tired signs are seen and sleep requirements gradually reduce.

It is best to be guided by your own baby's tired signs rather than a strict routine, after all trying to make a baby sleep when they are not tired is unhelpful as is keeping a tired baby awake until a specified sleep time as they will become over tired and more difficult to settle.

Night time is just feed/sleep routine, avoid eye contact with your baby as they will often smile at you and begin communication which stimulates them and makes it more difficult to get them back to sleep. Keep lights low or use a lamp or night light. Having a feeding chair in the room can help as this helps you to get him back into her cot soon after feeding and distinguish these feeds from day feeds which may be in the living area.

Sleep associations

These are associations between sleep and something else, for instance if your baby always falls asleep feeding, they learn that that is how to fall asleep. It is a beautiful thing to have your baby fall asleep feeding or in your arms but if this is the way they always fall asleep, then you will need to continue to do it every time. This also becomes a problem in light sleep if your baby looks around and finds he is in his cot now and not your arms he will cry out and ask for you to help him back to sleep, and that could be every 20–40 minutes due to their sleep cycle. I have to tell you that this is not much fun and this is the predicament I got in with my first baby, she had never slept more than two hours between feeds at five weeks of age, the only way I could get her to sleep was by breastfeeding and my husband had to rock her while pacing our hallway.

Sleep associations dependant on adult:

- Breast/bottle feed
- Cuddle/rock
- Car ride/pram ride
- Dummy (parent must replace)

Breaking these associations before 12 weeks is easier.

Independent sleep associations:

- Replicated without adult intervention
- Music/white noise
- Bubbling fish tank
- Ceiling fan

Three to six months tired signs

By three months of age most babies will be showing tired signs after being awake for one and a half to three hours.

Older baby tired signs, as well as those mentioned for newborns:

- Grizzling/crying
- Unable to play with toys
- Demanding attention/clingy
- Fussy with feeding

Often have three daytime naps of one to two hours, night waking normal and up until six months feeding is still required by many babies. Many babies of this age have settled into a pattern of waking less often. The same settling strategies are used for this age group as with newborns.

Six to twelve months tired signs

You will often see tired signs after being awake two to three hours. Usually around six months babies start to have longer night time sleeps of six hours or more. Many still wake but may only require resettling from a parent, they may not require feeding. Day sleeps are still very important at this age, aiming for at least one hour to be well rested.

Many parents would like their baby to sleep independently all night at this age however this is often a gradual process, implementing some of the strategies discussed may improve this however some babies are not ready. Other families are happy to wake overnight and feed their baby after six months and that is also fine, in fact many mothers tell me this is their special time with their baby and they have the best breastfeeds and time together due to no other distractions.

By six months of age babies understand that even though mum is gone, she still exists and will come when they cry, they understand that you love them and most babies have a secure attachment by this age. However it can sometimes feel as if they are using this knowledge against you. By eight months many babies display symptoms of separation anxiety and this can increase the problem.

If you are having some sleep problems I do not advocate the 'cry it out' method but there is nothing wrong with coming back and forth to a crying, grizzling and tired baby in a responsive way. It is a good idea to put them into their cot, after all her needs have been met, she has been fed, nappy changed, in a darkened room, showing tired signs and had some quiet wind down time as discussed earlier and then give her a chance to go to sleep herself. She may surprise you and do this well or she may cry and let you know that she needs some help. If your baby has not learnt the skill of falling asleep on her own, no matter what age, she will need some help to learn this, consistency and persistence are important so she can learn this new skill. It is important to really listen to your baby and try to

decide what she needs – is it just a grizzle and some grumpy 'talking', or is she in need of you in the room, hands on?

Staying and patting at this age has less success, many babies just want you to pick them up and to play with you so reduce eye contact as able. Try leaving the room and listening to the cries – by being responsive to the type of cry we can often allow baby to fall asleep themselves. If your baby is very distressed it is unlikely she will fall asleep and stay asleep. But if your baby is close to 'dropping off' to sleep and you go in, this may disturb her and she may think you are going to pick her up and then wake up again.

Occasionally nothing is going to work and then I suggest taking your baby for a walk in the pram, the crying is not as loud when you are outside and the pram ride and vibration just might put her to sleep. Make sure you use the pram harness so that if she does fall asleep you can leave her to nap in the pram close by when you return home.

If your baby is crying in distress whenever you put her into her cot, or waking repetitively during the night and these strategies are not helping, please seek help from your child health nurse, GP or paediatrician, who may be able to refer you to local services that specialise in sleep and settling – see parenting centre list in the resource section at the end of the chapter. You do not have to live this way and I have seen it many times taking a toll on entire families. Some time and effort will be needed to change this but it is worth it. If you are embarking on trying to improve sleep problems you also need to be kind to yourself, if able try to cook some meals ahead, ask friends and family for help and support and don't plan any major outings so that you can focus on sleep for a few days in a row with consistency.

Phasing out night feeds

If you are considering phasing out night feeds it is important that your baby be over six months, growing well and healthy. If breastfeeding over five minutes per feed, then you could try reducing feeding time each night by a few minutes until it is less than five. This may take a week or more to achieve, then don't offer them a feed, use your chosen settling strategy, as discussed earlier. Some families find it easier if the father attends to the baby for the first few nights as the baby will not expect a breastfeed.

If bottle feeding, you can reduce the quantity in the bottle every night until it is less than 50 ml and then stop offering the bottle and use settling strategies.

At first your baby may be upset and cry when they realise they are not getting a feed, but over time, usually only a few nights, they will settle down and hopefully stop waking overnight for a feed. If you are going to implement this, it is important to have consistency and persistence and not give in to your crying baby.

Co-sleeping with your baby

This is when your baby sleeps with you such as in your bed, on a couch or in your arms when you have fallen asleep, all of these situations present the same risks of fatal sleep accidents.

Red Nose and other sleep experts recommend that your baby sleep in a cot in your room for the first 6–12 months, this recommendation is based on years of research and significantly reduces the incidence of sudden unexpected death in infancy (SUDI) such as a fatal sleep accident or SIDS.

However many parents choose to sleep with their baby for cultural reasons or because they enjoy it, feel it improves the bonding relationship and makes their baby feel more secure. Many sleep with their baby out of desperation for sleep themselves, I know I have been there too.

Whatever the reason there are some guidelines which can reduce the risks involved:

- Always sleep your baby on her back.

- Sleep your baby in a safe sleeping bag and remain free of all adult bedding such as doonas and pillows.

- Bed must be firm, no water beds of woollen underlays.

- Place baby on the outside of the bed, not between two adults where bedding is more likely to cover her and get too hot.

- Put a barrier on the side of the bed so baby can't roll out.

If choosing to sleep with your baby out of desperation because they are unsettled then the concern is that you will not have set up your bed in the safest manner, please try to use the same principles. The other problem with this is that your baby will learn to sleep with you and it will be difficult to transition them back to sleeping in their cot. Often parents find it hard to agree on sleep methods for their baby, it is important to keep the lines of communication open.

If you are only co-sleeping because of exhaustion it is best to look at some other settling strategies to help your baby learn to sleep in their cot. After reading this chapter, try some of the strategies and then see the resource section for more sleep resources.

It is always best to sleep your baby on a separate sleep surface such as a cot or bassinet in the parents room.

Increased risks of SUDI (sudden unexpected death in infancy) and co-sleeping:

- If either parent is a smoker.

- If either parent is affected by alcohol or drugs, particularly sedating drugs.

- If either parent is sleep deprived or exhausted.

It is best not to co-sleep in these situations.

Chapter 7: Crying, sleep and settling

Summary

Sleep is a common challenge for the majority of parents and babies at some time or other throughout the first few years; please ask for help if it is becoming a problem, the earlier you intervene the quicker the problem is solved for you and your baby. Remember even a baby who sleeps well most of the time will have disturbed sleep when she has a cold virus or is teething but it will not last forever, try to go back to his normal pattern as soon as possible so that bad habits don't form. Remember that some baby's sleep better than others just as some adults sleep better than others. Some methods work better for some baby's and family's and sometimes you just need to cut yourself some slack, this period will not last forever, you will get through this but you don't have to do it on your own.

Websites

- Raising Children Network, The Australian Parenting website has many sleep resources, fact sheets and videos all evidence based and safe – raisingchildren.net.au

- Red Nose (formally SIDS & Kids) – many safe sleeping resources and information statements, evidence based, includes the Information Statement: Sleeping position for babies with gastro-oesophageal reflux (GOR) – rednose.com.au

- SIDS and Kids New Zealand – Safe sleeping information and advice, iPhone app, other language information – sidsandkids.org.nz

Early parenting centres around Australia

Australian Capital Territory	
Queen Elizabeth II Family Centre	(02) 6207 9977 (Community Health Intake)
New South Wales	
Karitane	(02) 9794 2300 or 1300 227 464 (Karitane Careline)
Tresillian Family Care Centres	(02) 9787 0855 (Sydney callers) or 1800 637 357 (regional callers)
Northern Territory	
The Northern Territory doesn't have parenting centres, but you can call Parentline on 1300 301 300 for support and advice on early parenting issues.	
Queensland	
Ellen Barron Family Centre	(07) 3139 6500
South Australia	
Torrens House	1300 733 606 (Child and Family Health Service)
Women's and Children's Health Network	(08) 8161 6003
Tasmania	
Parenting Centre – North (Launceston)	(03) 6434 6201
Parenting Centre – North West (Burnie)	(03) 6434 6201
Parenting Centre – South (Hobart)	(03) 6233 2700
Victoria	
O'Connell Family Centre	(03) 8416 7600
Queen Elizabeth Centre	(03) 9549 2777
Tweddle Child and Family Services	(03) 9689 1577
Western Australia	
Ngala Family Resource Centre	(08) 9368 9368 (Perth callers) or 1800 111 546 (regional callers).
Check with your Child Health Nurse, GP or Paediatrician for local sleep services.	

Chapter 8

Play and development

Chapter 8

Play and development

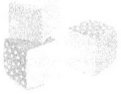

> *"Enjoy the magic of the first smiles from your baby."*
> **Belinda Joyce**

Play and Development

It is amazing to most new parents how their baby develops, in the first year alone most babies go from mainly sleeping, eating and pooping to crawling or even walking and saying some words! Each time your baby does something for the first time it will probably make you feel proud. Try not to compare your baby with other babies, the most important part of development is that there is gradual progress. If your baby does not seem to be progressing like other babies of a similar age, it is important to discuss this with your child health nurse, GP or paediatrician. We know parents' concerns are important as you are your own baby's expert.

Your amazing newborn, birth to three months

Your baby's brain is developing at a very fast pace within the first year, it develops through interaction and stimulation. All babies develop at their own pace however there are certain milestones that most will achieve around the same age.

Sight: At birth, your baby can see you well if cradled in your arms (20–40 cm away) anything further away will be blurred. His favourite thing to look at is his parents' or carers' faces, even better if they are smiling and

speaking to him in a kind voice, this is his first toy! He will also have a preference for looking at contrasting colours, black and white is most interesting for him. So toys, pictures, books with contrasting colours are well liked.

Hearing: He has already heard your voices often throughout the later months of pregnancy and he will recognise these as comforting. Babies have a preference for high-pitched voices and most adults automatically begin to speak this way with their baby. He won't like loud sudden sounds. Newborns will often turn their head toward a sound, a parent's voice, bell ringing, it is a delayed response but they will search for the source of the noise.

Touch: Babies love skin-to-skin contact, this often comes from breastfeeding but bottle feeding parents can do this too, even a simple carry pouch that allows your baby to be against a parent can work well. In the special care nursery we always encourage parents to put their premature baby skin to skin with them, research shows they grow and develop faster with this kangaroo care. All babies can benefit from this and it helps to create a strong emotional bond. Showering together is another chance for close skin to skin contact that many parents and babies enjoy.

Touch and physical contact is enjoyed and gentle baby massage is a wonderful activity to share with your baby. You can take a class to learn the techniques or even just try it yourself, if the baby enjoys it then it is fine. Using some massage oil will enhance the feelings of pleasure and probably make your baby feel drowsy and ready for sleep. Research shows that baby massage can help both parent and baby relax and calm irritability, improve colic and constipation, encourage longer and deeper sleep, is a great way for fathers to spend quality time with their baby, enhance a strong secure attachment which often continues into childhood and beyond. To find an infant massage class near you: infantmassage.org.au

Reflexes

Your baby will be born with many primitive reflexes which help to protect him:

- **Searching/rooting reflex:** If the baby's cheek is touched he will open his mouth and start to look around for the nipple to feed even if he is not hungry.

- **Sucking reflex:** when the roof of his mouth is touched he will begin to suck.

- **Palmer grasp reflex:** If you put your finger into his palm he will grasp a hold quite tightly.

- **The startle or moro reflex:** is when they have a fright such as hearing a loud sound or feeling like they are falling their arms will fly outwards, hands open, arch their back then arms come back in like an embrace. This reflex usually lasts from four to six months of age.

- **Stepping reflex:** If you stand your baby up fully supported and place his feet on the floor or surface he will begin to step with one leg then the other, even though he cannot hold up his own weight.

- **Babinski/plantar reflex:** If you stroke your baby's foot from heel to toe, his toes will push upwards and his foot will turn inwards.

These primitive reflexes will gradually reduce and be replaced by more voluntary responses over the coming months. These reflexes will be checked at birth by your midwife or doctor and then by your child health nurse.

Activities that help your baby to develop

Communication: Newborns have the ability already to hold gaze with you for short periods of time and will sometimes copy your facial expression, including poking out their tongue if you do. This early communication will grow into cooing in the first few weeks of life where your baby will hold eye contact and make cooing sounds or as many parents tell me, noises that sound like farm animals. In these early conversations, your baby will be quiet listening when you talk back and then when you finish he will 'talk' to you again. Most parents do this instinctively and it tells your baby that you are interested in their thoughts/feelings and that you care about him, he will continue to 'talk' to you more and more with positive reinforcement. Early on this may only last for short periods but as your baby grows they will become longer and longer and develop into conversations, he is actually learning how to take turns in conversations, tone and rhythm. By eight weeks of age you may find him gurgling, cooing and giggling to get your attention at times.

Singing: Babies love it when you sing to them, it does not matter what you are singing, nursery rhymes, the latest songs on the radio, anything... If you have forgotten nursery rhymes try watching a children's television show such as Playschool, they will all come flooding back, words and all. There are also many recordings you can purchase if you wish. If you don't like your own voice, don't worry your baby will! Add some movement perhaps rocking in your arms and you will see his enjoyment.

Smiling: By six weeks most babies have started smiling, at first it may just be in their sleep or when content but by six weeks most will smile while looking into your eyes in response to your smile. Most babies will do this when you are smiling at them and talking in a high-pitched voice, being more animated than usual helps as well. This is a very special achievement as it makes you feel special and all the hard work you have been doing may now feel like it is appreciated and you are getting something back for all your efforts.

Tummy time: This can start from birth, often this occurs on your chest when you're lying down, your baby will want to lift his head to look at your face. Even a newborn baby can lift his head up when on his tummy. It is important to do this from early in your baby's life as their head grows very quickly and becomes heavy, the longer you wait it becomes more difficult to lift and then he may dislike tummy time. Even as a newborn he will be able to lift his head and turn to the other side, by eight weeks he should be able to lift his head and hold his chin up off the floor, this only occurs with practice so keep giving him plenty of tummy time as practice.

The safest place for tummy time is on the floor as one day he will learn to roll and we don't want him to fall. Place a bunny rug or mat down on the floor. Put some interesting toys around him to look at, toys with mirrors are good. Lay down or sit next to him and talk. Gradually extend the time on his tummy. If he falls asleep put him in his cot on his back, don't let him sleep on his tummy as it is a sudden infant death syndrome (SIDS) risk, see the 'crying, sleep and settling' chapter for further details.

If he dislikes tummy time you can try other positions that will help those same muscles to strengthen such as lying him across your lap on his tummy when sitting, carrying him on his tummy across your arm, bathing him across your arm in the bath, massaging his back so he will tolerate some tummy time.

Head and neck control will gradually increase as your baby grows, this will be enhanced by tummy time also. Your baby will be able to track moving objects by around eight weeks.

Screen time: When playing on the floor remember there is no benefit to your baby's development with screen time, particularly large amounts of it. If there are older siblings it may be difficult to avoid some screen time but try to choose a place in the room not in front of the television, perhaps facing away from the screen, as your baby moves more this may become difficult. The television can be quite confusing for your baby and over-stimulate them making sleep more difficult.

Other screens such as mobile phones, tablets and computers are not suitable for this age group.

Play: Play is the natural way for babies to learn, however some adults need a reminder of how to play, particularly with a young baby and if you have not been around many babies this is something new to learn. Play for a young baby may just be talking to them while you change their nappy or sitting next to them on the floor while they have a kick around.

Babies don't need many toys and don't believe some of the claims on packaging, no toy will make your child a genius. Toys give you an opportunity to play with your baby, at the beginning he can't play with it himself, you can show him that when he shakes a rattle it makes a rattle sound, one day he will shake it himself. Always check toys are suitable from birth as they will be safe for your baby and not have small pieces that could be swallowed or choking hazards.

Take your baby outside, let them see and hear what is going on, trees, garden, cars driving. A walk in the pram is a chance to see new things and to learn.

You are your baby's favourite toy, time with you will be when his best learning experiences will happen.

Reading: It is never too early to start reading to your baby, he will enjoy this quiet time with you, maybe you could build this in before bedtime. Sit him on your lap with the book towards him, you don't have to read the words, you can point to pictures and tell him about what you can see.

See your child health nurse, doctor or paediatrician if your baby is:

- Not watching your face and making eye contact.
- Crying a lot and you are worried by this.
- Not making some cooing or animal-like noises.
- Not closing his eyes to bright light.

- Not moving his arms and legs around.

- Not feeding well.

- Not smiling by two months.

- Not looking at his hands by two months.

- Not focusing on you or objects by two to three months.

- Not supporting his head well.

- Not looking like he is hearing loud noises.

- Keeping his hands in a fist most of the time by three months of age.

Three to six months

Communication: Conversation is still one of the most important interactions for your baby's development, he will learn more about this with practice, talk to him throughout the day, tell him what you are doing, where you are going, how much you love him. He will talk back more and more over time as he gets better at it. He will turn his head towards sounds, especially your voice.

Movement: Many babies this age can push up on their arms while on their tummy. They will enjoy looking at their own hands like they are a toy, they will put their hands together and whack at hanging toys as well as hold a light rattle. By four months most babies will start rolling from front to back and back to side. Some will even be able to get all the way from back to front, although this is more challenging to get over their shoulder. In the early days most rolls are accidental, from his tummy, as he gets stronger, he will learn to put his arms out in front of him and then all he needs to do is tilt his head slightly and he will fall over. Reminder not to ever leave him on the change table unattended as he is likely to roll off and fall. If your baby is not rolling by four months give him plenty of tummy time to help him strengthen his muscles ready for rolling.

Chapter 8: Play and development

Most four-month-old babies can bear a little weight on their legs and may push up off your lap when you are sitting, this is good practice for him but he is not yet ready to take all of his weight.

By five months of age your baby can see bright colours better and will play with both his hands and feet.

Play: By around three months of age most babies can grasp and shake a rattle, they often drop them and need you to replace back in their hands. There are some rattling toys that you can Velcro onto your baby's wrist or attached to socks that your baby may enjoy, mine did.

Other toys that are made of different fabrics with different textures, some crinkly and some soft and smooth can be interesting for your baby. If he has a play gym that has hanging toys he can probably hit many of the toys now and watch them swing. Plenty of floor play time is beneficial. Bath time is a great time for play with toys or even just a small container to tip water from is fun.

See your child health nurse, doctor or paediatrician if your baby is:

- Not lifting his head up when on his tummy.
- Not enjoying eye contact with you and following moving objects with his eyes.
- Not responding to your speech with his own 'talking'.
- Crossing his eyes much of the time, occasionally is normal or one turned in or out eye.
- Not able to keep head up in a sitting position on your lap.
- Not reaching and grasping onto toys as well as putting them in his mouth.
- Not rolling by 5 months.
- Not able to sit with assistance.

Six to nine months

Communication: At six months, conversation has become more babbling with some single and double syllables, and by eight months maybe some real sounds such as Dadad, Bubub, sometimes even Mumum – usually repetitive and with no real meaning at this age, everything may be Dadad. This is a great opportunity to insist that the baby is calling for your partner to change him or her. Most babies find making the Dadad sound easier so Mums don't be disheartened if Mumma isn't his first word.

He may imitate sounds he hears you say. Laughing and giggling as well as screaming in delight or annoyance are common from six months also.

Movement and play: By around six months most babies can roll in both directions and sometimes do a few rolls together to get what they want. They will kick strongly when lying on their back which will sometimes hit you in the stomach when on the change table. They may push themselves along the floor in a caterpillar like action or even scoot backwards on their tummy or back. Floor play time is important to learn these new skills.

He can probably pass a toy from one hand to the other and will most likely put everything in his mouth to suck or chew. This is another way your baby learns about the world.

By eight months of age most babies can sit without support but there are some babies that are too busy rolling or crawling around the floor and don't want to stop and sit, don't worry about this they will probably learn this skill soon and floor play is more important. By nine months he will be able lean forward to pick up a toy while sitting.

Many babies enjoy 'posting' games where you give them a container of some sort and they put toys in and then take them back out. An empty tissue box works well.

Some babies are still rolling and wriggling around the floor while many babies can crawl around eight to nine months of age and some will start to pull themselves up on furniture – do stay close as they are likely to fall and given their head is the heaviest part it is what usually hits the floor first.

Now that he is more on the move you need to baby-proof your home further, get down on all fours and crawl around to see it from his perspective to look for dangerous objects.

Reading: Don't forget to read to him regularly even just for a few minutes each day. Just opening the book and pointing to the pictures and telling him what you see if usually enjoyed. No need to read large amounts of text, maybe it is a chance to show him animals and tell him what noise they make or the noise of a car. Board and cloth books are great at this age as he is likely to chew it.

Stranger anxiety/danger: Has usually developed by eight months and this can be quite subtle, just cuddling in a little closer to you when you are talking to someone new or less familiar or crying loudly when handed to a grandparent. It seems to be worse with tall males with loud voices and facial hair. This is a window in age where friends and family's babies don't like my husband even though he is great with babies and children, they cry and won't go to him for a cuddle or smile back at him, he doesn't take it to heart, as he is a big, loud man it is just their normal development. This will likely continue for some months and may get worse before it improves. This is not your baby being naughty, it is an inbuilt safety mechanism so that your baby knows who they know well and can trust. Your baby understands that even though you are not visible you still exist, playing peekaboo games helps him to understand this.

See your child health nurse, doctor or paediatrician if your baby is:

- Not giving you good eye contact and trying to have conversations with you, just his own language or babble.

- Not rolling.

- Not turning towards sounds and voices.

- Not sitting or standing with assistance.

- Unable to roll.

- Using one side of his body more than the other.

- Not able to swallow puree foods.

- Not showing affection for parents or carers.

- Not showing emotion such as a smile when happy.

- Stiff or floppy in tone.

Nine to twelve months

Conversations and interactions at this age are often your baby asking what's okay and what's safe for him to touch or do as he explores the world. He will repeat things that make you laugh such as blowing raspberries at you, even with a mouth full of food. If you say "no" to something he is likely to smile at you and do it anyway, not to be naughty but to test out what happens next, if it is a safety concern you may need to physically stop him doing it. If not, simple ignoring (at least he thinks you are) often works well.

Play: He will have favourite toys, games and activities but do continue to try new ones. Play outside as well as inside, he will probably love the outdoors, watching trees sway in the breeze, seeing animals such as ducks in a pond, watching cars. Gardening and yard work is intriguing and getting a little dirty is fun, just don't put his best clothes on.

You can try giving him a crayon or pencil and paper to 'draw'; do supervise as he will likely try to bite the crayon.

Some babies are into everything while others are happy to watch, whichever yours is will determine the level of safety equipment needed in your home.

Separation anxiety: He may cry when you leave the room even for short periods, separation anxiety is very common, he does not know when you are coming back and fears you will leave for a long period of time. Try to

tell him what you are doing and that you will be back soon, you can even keep speaking to him from another room so he at least has your voice to calm him. If you need to leave him with someone else remember that his crying is to try to keep you there but he will most likely stop soon after you have gone with some gentle distraction. This may happen even when one parents goes out and leaves the baby with the other parent, it's important not to take this personally, your baby may be used to being with one of you more often and therefore has a preference at present. Babies of this age really know who they know well and who is a stranger.

Movement: Most babies of nine months can stand holding onto something however until he can pull himself up it is best to keep weight bearing to occasional only as his hips, knees and ankles may not be ready. He will also begin 'cruising' around furniture soon.

Most babies will be crawling, rolling or pulling themselves along in some way by this age.

He will bang toys together which can get very noisy and enjoy eating with his hands, finger foods are great at this age as even with no teeth he can chew very well given practice.

Most babies by ten months of age can wave bye-bye to people and point to things of interest. He will probably enjoy bouncing to music either sitting or standing. Sing to him often he will love it even if you don't like the sound of your voice.

He will develop a pincer grip to pick things up with pointer finger and thumb, he may even pick up tiny pieces of fluff from your carpet even just after vacuuming!

By 12 months of age many babies continue to crawl or bottom shuffle, some can take a few independent steps or are getting close. Most babies will be pulling themselves up to standing on furniture or using your leg, he should be able to take his own weight to stand. Many can imitate actions like blowing a kiss.

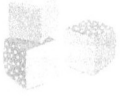

Communication: By 12 months of age babies will often say "no" by shaking their head. We would expect them to be saying at least two clear words by this age but some are saying many more, he will understand many more before he can say them. By 12 months he should understand simple instructions such as "give that to mummy" – that does not mean he will give it to you. Talk to him all day about what you are doing, what you can see, how proud of him you are, how much you love him.

At 12 months, he will be able to use a spoon to feed himself, it will be messy to start with but with practice he will get better, try using thicker foods to start with such as yoghurt and mashed potato as these stick to the spoon well.

By 12 months see your child health nurse, doctor or paediatrician if your baby is:

- Not pulling up on furniture to stand.
- Not crawling.
- Not giving you good eye contact and trying to communicate.
- Not babbling.
- Not pointing or waving.
- Not trying to tell you what he wants.
- Not showing emotions.

It is truly amazing to watch your baby develop and grow from birth to 12 months of age, with so many special firsts and feel proud when new stages are reached. For many parents, each stage can also feel a little sad with a sense of loss as their little baby grows and becomes a toddler at 12 months. He needs to do this, and generally following the normal stages of development is important for his future development.

Chapter 9

Getting out and about with your baby

Chapter 9

Getting out and about with your baby

> "A person's a person, no matter how small."
>
> **Dr Seuss**

Getting out and about with your baby

Getting out and about with your baby is an integral part of re-establishing some 'normality' in your routine and, for some, may require some planning as you need to make sure you have everything with you that your baby may need. The truth is you can literally pick up and go if you want but as you become more experienced with your new baby you realise pretty quickly that life is a lot easier when you are out and about with some key accessories. Many parents find this easier to do the night before, lay out your clothes, baby's clothes, have the nappy bag packed, anything important in the nappy bag such as child health record book if seeing the nurse or paediatrician.

I recommend you keep the nappy bag packed at all times then you can still have some spontaneity when someone invites you unexpectedly, this will give you more freedom.

Factor an extra 15 minutes into getting ready to go, you will need it. Sometimes you just have to go home when you have used the last nappy or your baby has vomited all over your clothes.

What to take in the nappy bag

- At least five nappies
- Change mat
- Wipes (small travel pack)
- Nappy cream if using
- Plastic bags for dirty nappies or clothes
- Two outfits (jumpsuits are easy)
- Hat
- Soft jacket/cardigan
- Dummy if using
- Tissues small pack
- Antibacterial hand gel for after nappy changes
- Bottles if using and formula powder
- Bunny rugs/blanket for playing on, for warmth if cold
- Cloth nappies or burp cloths for over shoulder if needed
- Purse/wallet
- Mobile phone
- Keys
- Snacks for parents

As your baby gets older:

- Snacks/food for baby
- Non-spill sippy cup of water
- Plastic spoon
- Toys
- Band-Aids
- Sunscreen

There is only so much you can fit in the nappy bag but you should keep another small bag in the boot of the car with backup nappies and clothes, including an outfit for yourself just in case a nappy leaks onto you or your baby vomits down your front, trust me it will happen. I distinctly recall my lovely first baby 'power pooing' or that is what we called it, through her nappy and jumpsuit and all over my jeans. We were out of town at the time and fortunately visiting family and able to borrow some clothes, it was clear that I needed to keep a spare set in the car.

Car safety: It is best to have your car restraint professionally fitted at an approved fitting station, see your local road traffic authority for locations. When driving with baby you may need to pull over occasionally to meet your baby's needs, especially on long trips, perhaps she has dropped her dummy or she is crying with distress. It is likely that she will sleep while the car is humming and vibrating along. Using a window shade will reduce the chance of sunburn and allow your baby to be more comfortable in bright light. Make sure the harness is firmly fitted for safety. Hanging toys can be helpful over the restraint for baby to look at.

Groups

Look around your area and see what types of groups are available, ask your child health nurse, GP, local council, neighbourhood and community health centre. Some areas have groups for specific communities such as young parents, Aboriginal and Torres Strait Islander families, families with multiples, rainbow families, grandparents, fathers and multicultural groups.

Groups are not for everyone, you may have an informal group of friends that you catch up with regularly or you may prefer just visiting one friend and their children at a time and that is fine. You may prefer to meet at a café for a cuppa or going for a walk with the prams together. Giving yourself and your baby chances for social connection and avoiding isolation is beneficial to most parents.

First time parent groups or mothers' groups: These are often run by your child health nurse and are a great way to meet other parents with babies of a similar age. In Victoria these often run for six to eight weeks, meeting once a week and start out by having some educational topics covered either by the nurse or guest speakers. You will all have a new baby in common and so always have plenty to talk about.

These often turn into an informal playgroup, sometimes they meeting at each other's homes until the babies are getting on the move, then it may be time to look for a larger venue. This is when it may be worth turning

into a more formal playgroup. See Playgroup below. Some groups meet for many years and some lifelong friendships can be made.

MOPS (mothers of pre-schoolers) also run some groups these are organised by a church group however you do not need to be involved with the church to enjoy these. Even though it is called MOPS they often have mothers of young babies and all the way up to kindergarten age children.

Walking groups meet and go on a walk with prams together, this is a chance for both some social connection and exercise.

Mother and baby exercise classes: an opportunity to exercise with your baby.

Playgroups

Playgroups are a more formal regular gathering of parents and babies, children, mums, dads, grandparents and carers are all welcome. Activities include, indoor play, outdoor play, music and singing, reading, art and craft, group outings. Usually they are held at the same venue weekly at the same time. Often the venues are community halls/centres, child health centres, women's centres, preschools, kindergartens and schools. Some playgroups are stand alone and set up by the participants which means you may have to help running the group sometimes, while others are facilitated by community groups, local council or other agencies and they arrange it, set it up and pack up.

Parents or carers stay and mix with each other, supporting the babies and children to interact together often forming their own friendships and benefiting from the social side of playgroup. All babies and children from birth to school age are welcome to take part. When looking for a playgroup it is good to ask around and to try to find one that has children of a similar age to your own.

Playgroup is a great way to make new friends especially if you are new to the area. And if you are at all like me with our first baby I made myself

a little housebound. It took both my mother and husband to encourage me to get out more and going to a playgroup was as much for me to interact with other parents as it was for our daughter to engage with other children. Research has shown that playgroup benefits a child's development including physical, social, emotional, language, cognitive and communication.

Library story time

Most libraries run preschool story time groups and some have groups such as rhyme time and baby bounce. These groups are usually free and promote a love of books and reading as well as being a chance for social contact for both baby's and parents. Check with your local library for details. There is no commitment required, if you can't make it one week you just don't go.

Other outings

Try to get out of the house at least every few days, even a quiet walk around the block with your baby in the pram can make you feel so much better. Your baby will often be distracted when out of the house and interested in the world around him.

Travel

Change your baby's nappy just before leaving on a plane, bus, train, car, ship and before going for a walk.

Car travel: Is common in Australia as it is often the case we are driving several hours to see family, try to stop and take your baby out of the car restraint every two hours if possible, allow her to stretch. This may mean longer travel times and a need to stop over along the way. Sun shades are very helpful in the car and allow your baby to sleep as well as reduce the chance of sunburn. Hanging toys can help on a long trip as well as familiar music and your voice. You must stop if you are removing your baby from the restraint to feed, it is illegal and unsafe to travel with your baby not strapped in.

Chapter 9: Getting out and about with your baby

Overseas: If leaving Australia you will need a passport for your baby. If travelling by plane, ask what assistance they will provide for a baby, often you are able to get a bassinet and special seating that offers a little more space. Some airlines will allow more luggage to accommodate strollers, portable cots and other necessary items. Feed your baby on take-off and landing if possible or use a dummy, as the sucking helps to equalise the pressure and allow their ears to 'pop', minimising discomfort and the likelihood of a crying baby.

Consider where you are travelling to and if you will have access to clean water for making up bottles if required. Will you need to take some food from home for your baby or will it be a problem in customs. Are any other immunisations required in the country you are visiting?

Pack plenty of clothes for your baby, consider weather at destination, layers often work well. Bring familiar toys that your baby likes and can help to distract him but be careful not to take loud annoying toys for other travellers.

Try to stick with a similar routine if possible when you arrive, however this is not always possible.

We have only ever taken our babies on flights within Australia with four hours being the longest and they have been okay for most of the trips, with feeding them on take-off and landing we got through. Clients have shared mixed experiences with me ranging from very young babies who fed and slept most of the trip, even long international flights, to parents of older babies who wanted to be able to crawl around and unfortunately that is not possible on a plane. You and your family's situation will determine the best way to travel and it shouldn't be stopped by having a baby, but more thought and organisation may be required.

Getting out and about with your baby is important, you will find ways that suit you and your baby.

Chapter 10

Parents' health and wellbeing

Chapter 10

Parents' health and wellbeing

> *"You will be a better parent if you try to look after yourself."*
>
> **Belinda Joyce**

Parents' health and wellbeing

In this new role of parenting it is important to not only look after your new baby but to also look after yourselves. Often parents, especially mothers are so busy caring for their baby that they forget about themselves but you will be a better parent and partner if you can look after yourself as well.

Mother's physical health in the early weeks

In the early weeks after the birth mother's bodies will gradually return to a pre-pregnancy state, the uterus will continue to shrink in size, decreasing vaginal bleeding will finish within the first six weeks and hormones will start to settle. If breastfeeding your breasts may remain larger but should become softer and more comfortable over the first few weeks.

Pelvic floor exercises are very important, do them regularly. If you are unsure ask your midwife, child health nurse or doctor how to do them correctly. If you have any incontinence (leaking of urine) please discuss this with your midwife, child health nurse or doctor, they may suggest seeing a women's health physiotherapist who specialises in this type of care. Incontinence is not something you should put up with, in many cases it can be corrected by doing targeted pelvic floor exercises and the earlier you seek help the better the outcome.

Many women feel some back pain often before and after birth but if this is not improving in the early weeks, see a physiotherapist for assessment.

Some gentle walking in the early days is beneficial, increase this gradually as comfort allows. This is not exercise to lose weight, this is just for your overall wellbeing.

A check-up six weeks after the birth with your GP, obstetrician or midwife is important to follow up on your health after the birth. It is a chance to discuss any problems since the birth that may not have resolved such as vaginal bleeding or discharge, stitches, urinary incontinence, constipation, back pain, mental health as well as contraception. Your doctor will also give your baby a physical examination and the first immunisations may be completed, often by the practice nurses. It is worthwhile writing down a list of questions that you may have about you or your baby otherwise you might walk away forgetting to ask a couple of your questions.

After six weeks most women are able to get back to their normal physical activities such as sport, start slowly and gradually build this up. Many find physical activity very beneficial both physically and mentally.

If you feel as though you have gained too much weight during the pregnancy avoid extreme dieting especially if you are breastfeeding. Talk to your GP about safe weight loss, many weight loss programs are suitable for breastfeeding mothers with some small alterations. Try not to compare yourself to the celebrities who seem to lose their baby weight and look fabulous within a few short months after their birth, it is best to do this gradually. Fad and restrictive diets are not a healthy way to reduce weight and may not give you and your baby, if breastfeeding, enough calories.

The new role of parenthood: Just like any new role it takes a little while to get used to becoming a parent especially if you are the primary carer. Try not to compare yourself to others, we all do things differently and that is normal.

Listen to your inner voice, most of the time it will help you make decisions, slow down and reflect, does it feel right, sometimes it may be silent and that is okay. You can always ask others for help in this new role.

Mummy guilt: I truly believe that all mothers want to do the best for their baby, unfortunately in our society there is too much judgement of mothers and this often comes from other mothers. Try not to take this on.

For some social media can add to this feeling, with pictures of mothers and babies appearing to always be having fun, having amazing outings, dressed in spotless name-brand clothes. Remember most people won't put a post on social media about the terrible day they are having or that their beautiful baby cries all day long and they don't know how to stop them. No one is a super mum even if it looks like it. On the other hand social media can be very positive in reducing the social isolation many new mothers feel.

Loss of identity: Many mothers feel a distinct loss of identity as a mum, I remember becoming known as 'Jasmine's mum' rather than Belinda and it was a shock. For many women they have at least temporarily lost their job title from work also.

Lack of control: Your baby probably won't fit into your schedule the way you thought she would, plans may be derailed at the last minute, it may be difficult to be on time, something you may have always been. Before having our first baby I clearly remember saying to my husband that I was going to love being a stay at home Mum because I would be able to get all the cooking and cleaning done while he was at work and then when he was home we would be able to have family time, I imagined a traditional role with a clean house, home-baked cookies and cakes and exquisite meals. As you know this was not the reality, often when he arrived home from work I would hand him a screaming baby and walk away to go and try to find enough ingredients to cook something for dinner.

For many women this lack of control can be difficult, especially if you have come from a profession where you had significant expertise and control.

Fathers and partners who return to work while their partner is home with the baby tell me it can be hard to leave them at home and go to work. The tiredness is difficult especially if commuting long distances as well as the need to help their partner when returning from a stressful day of work, they feel there is no downtime. Missing out on watching your baby grow and those firsts such as first smile, first roll over, first steps are often mentioned.

Typically fathers have great social pressure to provide for their family especially at this time and finances are often stretched from going down to one income. Sometimes mothers also feel the pressure to return to work early for various reasons such as financial necessity, they have their own business or for personal reasons. While mothers need time to recover from giving birth, in some families there is pressure for the mother to work or return to work while their partner stays home. See the 'Return to work' chapter.

Being the good enough parent: This is a term which I really like, there is no need to be a perfect parent, as long as you are trying to meet your baby and your own needs that's all you can do. Sometimes you will do better than others. I can remember calling my first baby a guinea pig, because I was testing new skills out on her but ultimately I did not know what I was doing much of the time, she seems to have turned out well so I must have done okay.

Remember it takes a village to raise a child, no one except maybe yourself thinks you have to do it all alone. Ask for help from friends and family, this is not a sign of weakness and in fact gives your baby more chance to socialise and make new relationships into the future.

With many families living in a different location to their parents the support from family can be more difficult, making close friends and support networks locally becomes even more important.

Parents working together: This is often a challenging time in any relationship, the birth of your baby has added many new tasks as well as deprived you of sleep; the baby needs to come first and this can make many partners feel unloved. On top of this many couples find they are not speaking very nicely to each other at this time and this can add to feelings of resentment. Try to be patient with each other, remember you are on the same side and it will get easier over time. Talk about it.

This time in your life raises many new experiences and you may be surprised about how your expectations of each other differ. We all come from different families with different experiences and therefore it is not unusual to assume that certain things will happen and then be surprised when it doesn't play out that way. For example who will stay home, for how long and what will be the role of each parent.

Try to come up with different jobs around the home that you can both do to keep things running smoothly. Make some time for each other by asking family or friends to babysit occasionally.

Mental health

Most women recover physically quite quickly after the birth of a baby although it can take some months to feel like yourself again.

Looking after your mental health:

- Lower your usual expectations about what you would like to achieve each day.

- Write a list of five to seven small tasks (have a shower, playtime with baby) that you would like to achieve and tick them off to obtain a sense of accomplishment.

- If possible try to shower first thing in the morning, and get dressed and prepared for the day.

- Plan your week to include time out visiting family and friends as well as time at home.

- Take your baby for a walk in the pram three or four times a week. This will help you and your baby to get some fresh air and exercise. This will also help reduce that feeling of being trapped in the house all day. You may even be able to arrange to meet a friend and walk together.

- Organise a menu plan and shop once a week, this will help you to feel more in control, especially towards the end of the day when you and baby are getting tired. You may even be able to prepare parts of the meal during the day or use a slow cooker to assist.

- Sit down and rest as often as you can, especially in the weeks following the birth.

- Try to take some time out for yourself at least once a week where your partner or family care for your baby and you can have some 'me time'. This may be just going to the local coffee shop and reading a book. Even time away for 30 minutes can assist your mood and overall wellbeing.

- Consider learning and practicing some form of mindfulness or relaxation strategies. There is considerable evidence that practicing mindfulness regularly improves our wellbeing, physical and mental health. There are a number of apps that you can download to assist. Mind the Bump and Smiling Mind developed by Beyond Blue are free to download and provide many good practices.

Many parents of new babies suffer from mental health symptoms, both women and men.

In the early days after birth around 80% of new mothers experience 'baby blues', feeling down and tearful which is thought to be caused by fluctuating hormones but this should pass quickly with no special treatment. However if either of you experience symptoms of depression or anxiety for more than two weeks or if these feelings are severe it is worth talking to a health professional such as your GP or Maternal, Child and Family Health Nurse, they can help to explain and reassure you, help you decide if treatment is required and give suggestions and possible referral to mental health professionals. We know that around one in every seven women will develop postnatal depression (PND) and that many men do as well, although the prevalence is unknown.

Symptoms of depression and anxiety – you may have one or more of these as they are different for everyone:

- Feelings of sadness, low mood or feeling numb.

- Feelings of anxiety about your baby's wellbeing.

- Difficulty sleeping even when the baby is asleep.

- Not finding joy in activities that you used to love.

- Not enjoying being with your baby.

- Fear of being alone with your baby.

- Panic attacks (shortness of breath, difficulty breathing, tightness in chest).

- Negative thoughts.

- Feeling guilty.

- Lack of appetite or over-eating.

- Lack of confidence.

- Staying home and not wanting to leave the house/avoiding social contact.

- Not looking after yourself.

- Not coping with regular routine daily tasks.

- Waking with a sense of fear and anxiety, dreading and feeling overwhelmed with the day ahead.

- Thoughts of self-harm or harming your baby (if you are at immediate risk of harming yourself or your baby call 000 for assistance in Australia).

Mental health support

- Suicide call back service 1300 659 467

- Lifeline 13 11 14

- Beyond Blue 1300 224 636 24 hours/ 7 days a week

- To chat online, email Beyond Blue or join the forum visit: https://www.beyondblue.org.au/get-support/get-immediate-support

- PANDA National Helpline 1300 726 306 Monday - Friday, 10am - 5pm

Websites:

- cope.org.au

- panda.org.au

- mensline.org.au

- relationships.org.au

Mental health services

Private and public services available.

Phone your local mental health team often located within public hospitals.

Specialised services such as:

St John of God Raphael Services in VIC: Ballarat, Bendigo, Berwick, Geelong. WA: Perth, Wembley, Fremantle, Midland and Cockburn. NSW: Blacktown.

Different services operate throughout Australia, discuss with your GP or child health nurse.

Treatments for Postnatal Depression

In most cases your GP will be able to refer you on to a psychiatrist or psychologist for care during this time, some of this may be Medicare funded. Some treatments include: medication, counselling and cognitive behaviour therapy which helps you to notice negative thought patterns common in PND and learn to turn them around.

Supporting someone with postnatal depression or anxiety

Talking to your partner about their and your own feelings is important as well as supporting them in getting appropriate mental healthcare.

Practical help, such as doing more of the housework, caring for other children, saying yes to those family and friends offering to help. Letting family and friends know what you are going through and asking for some extra support and then accepting this. Taking the baby out for a walk or to visit friends and letting your partner get some much needed sleep.

If you are able to take some leave from work to stay home to support your partner this can really help.

Intimacy

Many women do not feel interested in resuming sex for some weeks or months after having a baby. The tiredness and constant 24 hour care of a baby can be all consuming. Depending on the birth and any stitches or trauma involved it may require more time. Many partners are worried about hurting their partner during sex. It is important to take this slowly and to keep lines of communication open along the way, if you try and realise you are not ready then try again next week. After all there are other ways to be intimate and express your love than just sex. Even just talking to each other about your feelings and fears, cuddling and kissing, working together to care for your baby and each other can all help your relationship.

Discuss contraception needs with your doctor, even if you are fully breastfeeding and have not had a period you can sometimes conceive another baby. Many find condoms are good at the beginning for contraception depending on when you may want another baby.

Chapter 11

Returning to work

Chapter 11

Returning to work

> *"A baby fills a place in your heart that you never knew was empty."*
>
> **Anonymous**

Returning to work

The decision on whether or not to return to work is a very personal one and needs to be based on your own family, what suits one family will not suit another. Some women choose to stay at home while many women are returning to paid work earlier than in previous years for a number of reasons including, financial pressure, enjoying adult interaction at work, personal reasons, enjoying their work, it is seen as normal. Maternal employment has been gradually increasing in Australia over the last 30 years with many mothers returning to work in the first year of their baby's life.

Things you and your partner need to consider:

- Do you both want to work outside your home?

- Do you have some paid maternity leave and for how long?

- Who has the greater earning capacity?

- How flexible are your work arrangements, could you do some work from home or adjust start and finish times?

Chapter 11: Returning to work

- List all the jobs that need to be done both inside and outside the home, who will do what? Cooking, cleaning, laundry, shopping, working? This workload needs to be re-negotiated.

- How much money do you need? Do you have a budget?

- What feels right and what will make you happy?

Some families I see have made a bold choice to downsize their house and cars to enable one parent, often the mother, to work less or not at all. I have seen both parents scaling back and working part time, sharing the primary carer role equally, sometimes reducing or even avoiding the use of childcare completely. More fathers are staying home as the primary carer. If our circumstance were different, my own husband often says he would have liked to be a stay at home dad.

Being a full-time parent is a challenging role and one that is often misunderstood, it is the most challenging work you will ever do and unfortunately in our society, it remains largely unpaid and undervalued.

After having our first baby I felt grateful that I was able to stay home fulltime for over 12 months before gradually taking on some nursing shifts. As our family continued to expand I went back to university to become a midwife, something I had been wanting to do for many years. Although challenging with a baby and toddler, most clinical placements were completed on weekends and school holidays as my husband was home from work. Occasional childcare and family support provided some back up options too.

When I began my midwifery career and after the third and fourth children turned one, I returned to work two days a week. The children attended one day at a childcare centre each week and I worked one day each weekend when they could be with their father – he enjoyed this time with the children. This worked for us but like I said earlier, every family is different. This part-time work gave me the ability to spend time with our children most days and still participate in playgroups, kinder-gym,

swimming lessons and library story time sessions, not all at once of course. I did not feel like I was missing out and I could still progress in my career and contribute financially to our family.

In the majority of families I see, the mother returns to part-time work when their baby is somewhere between six months and 18 months of age – often this is when their leave expires and financial pressures require it. Many of these mothers tell me that they really enjoy their time at work, the adult conversation, keeping up with changes in their industry and using their brain in a different way, although it is often challenging to juggle both work and home life but the benefits often outweigh the difficulties.

Some parents even start a business during their maternity leave and then have flexibility and the ability to work from home, some are doing similar work while others try something completely new.

The key to successfully returning to work is planning ahead and trying to stay organised, it can often feel like a juggle.

Choosing care for your baby

When deciding on your childcare options it is important to find out what financial assistance you may be eligible for. In Australia childcare assistance can help to reduce the cost of childcare. Eligibility rules apply. Contact the Department of Human Services on 136 150.

You need to take into account the cost of childcare and make sure that this is covered by the money you will earn, some families find it is not worth returning to work financially.

Availability of childcare can also be a problem with some childcare centres having long waiting lists.

Some alternative childcare options include: a family member such as a grandparent either in your home or theirs, child carer or a nanny in your home, an occasional childcare centre, long day care centre or family day care in a carers home with other children.

Long day care is childcare provided in a centre that often opens early and closes late, allowing you to drop your baby off on your way to and from work. Opening hours between childcare centres vary, some cater for shift workers who start very early in the morning, others do not. Most have a baby room, toddler room and pre-schooler room, some even offer kindergarten or preschool options.

Family day care is childcare provided in the educators home and will be with a small group of children only, some may be the educators own children.

Occasional care is more suited to care only required occasionally for some time out or to attend appointments child free. This can work well for casual workers whose hours can be changeable or students. Services operate differently, our local service offers sessions of a few hours at a time up to full days.

It is a good idea to ask friends and family what they have used and to see what options are available in your area. Then contact the centres and ask if you can go and have a look at the facilities , your child can have a play while you are there and you can watch the staff interact with the children.

My advice is to see how you feel about each childcare option, after all you will be leaving your precious baby there regularly. Below are some questions you could ask yourself about each centre or service.

- Do the children look generally happy and their needs being met?

- Were the staff welcoming?

- Do you feel comfortable there?

- Was my own child settled in the centre?

- What sort of routine do they follow?

- Where will my baby sleep?

- Does the centre provide meals and snacks, check this week's menu?

- Does the centre provide nappies or do you supply them?

- Is there a kindergarten or preschool in the centre for future?

- Was the centre generally clean?

- Did the children have access to good quality toys?

- What qualifications do the staff have?

- What carer to child ratios do they use?

- Can I claim childcare benefit and rebate?

In large centres it is normal to see children with runny noses, particularly in winter as the staff do not have time to keep all the children's noses wiped at once, and there is no need to be concerned about this. If it is family day care do they need to take children to and from kindergarten or will your child be at the carers home all day. If it is occasional childcare, will you be able to book regularly enough for your work hours or will you need to look at a long day care centre?

Once you have decided on care it is a good idea to gradually get your baby used to going there – most childcare centres have an orientation program where you bring them in a few times and stay and play then start to leave them for a few hours at a time. Or if it is in your own home have the carer come in and start to get to know your baby and his routines.

Even after doing all of this research and choosing the best care available it is normal to still feel uneasy about leaving your child with others even if they are family. Many parents feel guilty about returning to work and not caring for their own baby even if they really want to head back to work because they love their job. For many it is an internal emotional struggle which can last some time, many mothers judge themselves far more harshly than anyone else does. Just know that you are doing what is right for your family, particularly if you have to work for financial reasons.

Chapter 11: Returning to work

Discussing your return to work with your employer

You need to negotiate your return to work date, how many days a week you will work as well as any family friendly options available, if any.

Some mothers find their previous fulltime role which they were planning to return to no longer suits, since having their baby they would prefer part-time work. In this case depending on the size of the organisation you may be able to negotiate a job share or a different role that can be part-time. You have the right to request flexible work arrangements including part-time work, changed start and finish times or work from home arrangements. Your employer can refuse these requests on reasonable business grounds such as reduced productivity, it would impact on other employees work arrangements or it is too costly.

All parents returning to work after unpaid parental leave are entitled to come back to the same job even if they have had a replacement in this position during your leave.

If you feel you are being treated unfairly please contact the Fair Work Commission 13 13 94.

Breastfeeding and return to work

Some mothers manage continuing to breastfeed for many months after returning to work by expressing and the carer feeding the baby with breastmilk in a bottle. It is good to plan this in advance and to gradually get a stockpile of frozen expressed breast milk to help with this transition. Try to get your baby used to taking the bottled expressed breast milk well before your first day at work, some babies won't take this from their mother as they prefer to breastfeed, have your partner or carer try.

Depending how often you have been breastfeeding your baby, you may need to express at work for comfort and to maintain your supply and this milk can be refrigerated and used for your baby the following day. Use an insulated bag and cold packs to help with transporting the expressed milk.

If you are unable to express enough breastmilk, the use of some formula while continuing to breastfeed is still beneficial. Some mothers choose to feed their baby formula when they are at work and continue to breastfeed when they are together with their baby, even if that is only before and after work during the week and on weekends.

When your baby is over six months of age his requirements for breastmilk will reduce as solid foods increase, this will reduce the amount of expressing required.

Look into what your employer can offer to assist you to continue to breastfeed, is there a breastfeeding policy, is there ABA Breastfeeding Friendly Workplace Accreditation (BFWA), can you take breaks to express, privacy, refrigerator to store breastmilk? Not allowing adequate facilities and breaks to breastfeed or express may constitute discrimination and may also breach health and safety laws.

Sick baby

In the first year of life your baby is likely to get many cold viruses as well as other illnesses – if using childcare she is likely to get many more due to mixing with more children. Childcare centres ask that you don't bring your child if unwell and more infectious illnesses have exclusion periods. If your baby has a temperature, rash, conjunctivitis, diarrhoea, vomiting, or is otherwise unwell they should stay home and rest. If your child has the common cold and is not terribly unwell she can probably still go to childcare as this can go on for many days.

Try to have a plan of what you will do if your baby is unwell and unable to go-to childcare – can grandparents or friends help out, which parent will take family leave? My husband and I share these based on what we have on at work that day, we use many more days of leave for our children than we ever use for ourselves. There never seems to be a good day to take off work but your child needs you more.

Chapter 11: Returning to work

Tips to manage return to work

Many parents find that with the return to work there is an increase in stress either from work or from managing the work life balance. Try to leave work problems at work and be present at home with your family.

- Try to take care of yourself, eat well and have some regular exercise, even just walking with the pram is beneficial.

- Many women find they are still doing the majority of domestic jobs even though they have returned to work. Trying to share the load with your partner can make a difference.

- Get organised the night before, bags packed and clothing chosen.

- Before returning you may be able to load the freezer with some meals that can be used after work or you may find a 'cook up' on the weekend takes the pressure off during the week.

- Regular time to yourself that is not work is important for both parents to help manage this, it may be as simple as taking an uninterrupted bath or a night out with friends or together without your baby.

- Finding routines for your family can help, babies and children thrive on routine.

Further Support:

- Raisingchildren.net.au
- Department of Human Services on 136 150
- www.humanservices.gov.au
- Fair Work Commission 13 13 94
- Fair work Ombudsman website: www.fairwork.gov.au
- https://www.fairwork.gov.au/leave/maternity-and-parental-leave/returning-to-work-from-parental-leave
- mychild.gov.au
- familydaycare.com.au
- echildcare.com.au

About the Author

Belinda Joyce

Author, Registered Midwife and Maternal and Child Health Nurse

Belinda loves working with families and assisting them on their journey to parenthood while also helping them to enjoy their babies and children. Belinda specialises in providing family-centred care. She also takes pride in having mentored many student nurses and midwives over the past 20 years.

Belinda has earned a Bachelor of Nursing, and Graduate Diploma of Midwifery, and a Master of Nursing Science in Child, Family & Community. Most of the time when she was studying she was raising her four young children.

Throughout her nursing and midwifery career of 20 years, Belinda has worked with many organisations. She has worked with thousands of parents and newborns during childbirth education, prenatal care, labour and birth, postnatal care and in the special care nursery with unwell or premature babies. She has also worked throughout regional Victoria with multiple local governments serving as a Maternal and Child Health Nurse and continues in this role where she performs home visits and key age consultations with families and children from newborn to school age including facilitating first time parent groups (mothers' groups).

Belinda's professional associations include the Victorian Association of Maternal & Child Health Nurses, Maternal Child and Family Health Nurses Australia and the Australian Nursing and Midwifery Federation.

As a mother of four children, Belinda enjoys being involved in all of their school activities. From performing the role of a classroom helper to volunteering for canteen, sports and fundraising activities, she sees her children as the greatest achievements in her life.

While fulfilling her dream to see the world, Belinda has travelled throughout Australia, England, France, Italy, Fiji, Thailand, Singapore and New Zealand.

Belinda Joyce is the author of *Survive and Enjoy Your Baby* and lives in Victoria, Australia with her husband and four children.

Recommended Resources

Visit

www.BelindaJoyce.com

for more resources including:

- Articles, blog and tools.

- Free tip sheets, checklists and printables to help with sleep and getting organised with parenting.

- Join my free weekly newsletter for all the most up to date information to help you enjoy your baby and your family.

Find out more about how to become part of Belinda's private members area for even more benefits:

- E-classes

- Expert interviews with health professionals

- Parenting self-care resources

- New resources added regularly

- Much more to come...

  Book Belinda as a speaker for your next event.

www.BelindaJoyce.com

red nose
saving little lives

There is no rulebook for parents. But there are facts. And that's the only thing we are interested in.

Join Red Nose Knows and we will:

- keep you up to date with evidence based advice on how to keep baby safe

- help you make informed choices about safe products

- send you information when you need it, as you need it

join red nose knows
rednose.com.au

www.ingramcontent.com/pod-product-compliance
Lightning Source LLC
Chambersburg PA
CBHW072005090426
42740CB00011B/2092